Winds of Change

Declaring War on Education

Darlene Leiding

ROWMAN & LITTLEFIELD EDUCATION
A division of
ROWMAN & LITTLEFIELD PUBLISHERS, INC.
Lanham • New York • Toronto • Plymouth, UK

KH

Published by Rowman & Littlefield Education
A division of Rowman & Littlefield Publishers, Inc.
A wholly owned subsidary of The Rowman & Littlefield Publishing Group, Inc.
4501 Forbes Boulevard, Suite 200, Lanham, Maryland 20706
www.rowman.com

10 Thornbury Road, Plymouth PL6 7PP, United Kingdom

British Library Cataloguing in Publication Information Available

Library of Congress Cataloging-in-Publication Data

Leiding, Darlene, 1943–
Winds of change : declaring war on education / by Darlene Leiding.
p. cm.
Includes bibliographical references and index.
ISBN 978-1-61048-821-1 (cloth : alk. paper) — ISBN 978-1-61048-822-8 (pbk. : alk. paper) — ISBN 978-1-61048-823-5 (electronic)
1. Public schools—United States. 2. Children with social disabilities—Education—United States. 3. School improvement programs—United States. I. Title.
LA217.2.L446 2011
370.973—dc23

2011049878

The paper used in this publication meets the minimum requirements of American National Standard for Information Sciences Permanence of Paper for Printed Library Materials, ANSI/NISO Z39.48-1992.

Printed in the United States of America

4/15/13

Contents

Foreword

There is no lack of books, articles, op ed pieces, speeches, tweets, letters to the editor, and other means of communication discussing the issues, problems, and needs in American elementary and secondary education. Academics, practitioners, politicians, pundits, think tank operatives, and concerned citizens all seem to be commenting on what is wrong and what needs to be done in our schools.

Unfortunately, the comments are not always useful for those who care about the continuous improvement in our school systems. For example, one can conclude that some academics appear to be motivated more by the need for promotion and tenure than concern for the education of our youth. Others who profess to be developing new theories of education are merely presenting thinly disguised ideologies as theory. Many politicians write to appeal to specific voting blocs in an effort to get or retain public office. What passes as research, whether on campus, in think tanks, or legislative bodies is akin to the "push polling" seen in public opinion sampling—selling a point of view rather than seeking the truth.

Yet, there are people who write with no motivation other than to use their knowledge, skill, and commitment to write about what they have learned from their training and experience. Darlene Leiding is one of those people. Drawing on her extensive experience and a passion for research she has made significant contributions to the literature with books such as *The Won't Learners: An Answer to Their Cry* and *Racial Bias in the Classroom*.

Dr. Leiding has the advantage of seeing education from many different perspectives. She has worked in a variety of settings—district schools, contract schools, and charter schools. She has been a classroom teacher, special education teacher, and school principal. She has demonstrated a special commitment to low income and diverse populations such as an American

Indian school, a school with all African American students, and teaching in a school were the majority of the students were in trouble with the law for drug use or criminal behavior. In short, she has seen it all. Coupling that experience with an enthusiasm for research and drawing on a variety of resources, Leiding has, through this book, made another significant contribution to an understanding of American education—where it is and where it might go.

This book is an easy read. Leiding's style is understandable, not encumbered with the pedantic writing often plaguing education books. Much like a good speaker who has an opening, the body of the speech, and a conclusion, she begins each chapter with a quote to stimulate thinking, launches into the substance of the chapter, and concludes with "Points to Remember."

Each chapter could stand alone as a paper on some aspect of education. There are plenty of facts, but they are used to illustrate points, not to overwhelm the reader. There are some arguments that all might not agree with, but Leiding appears willing to lay out propositions and then let the readers either defend other positions or agree with hers.

There is much historical information in the book and discussions of who influenced American education through the years, but the more important contribution is taking on contemporary issues such as federal education legislation, standardized testing, achievement gap, impact of the information age, English language learners, weapons and drugs in schools, and the deterioration of the family.

The last two chapters in the book deal with current and future trends. This challenges the readers to rethink how they are delivering education in order to give the greatest opportunity for all students. Everyone who reads this book will be a better educator having been challenged to examine what they know and what they are doing.

Bob Brown

Preface

Is school a "white" thing? If not, then why do so many students of color, even those from middle-class families, perform so badly in our classrooms? Why do young black students, born decades after the heyday of the Civil Rights movement, see themselves as victims? This appears to be the defining element of their existence.

Touted as an unsinkable ship of social progress for more than a century, public education is leaking badly. Achievement is stagnant or declining, public opinion is low, and community conflict over what should be taught seems to be increasing. Some schools, especially in the inner city, have already slid beneath the waves, extinguishing the educational hopes and dreams of countless children. Literally, thousands of would-be reformers have suggested patches here and there, but the water just keeps flooding in.

America's legacy to its young people includes bad schools, poor health care, deadly addictions, crushing debts, and utter indifference. We are constantly grappling with the concept of courage and related notions about fear and violence, sacrifice and being a scapegoat, imitation and exposure. We must continuously think about the common good.

If the education of the next generation is not to be completely forsaken, we need to cast aside our assumptions about how schools should be run, and consider not only major overhauls to the current system but entirely different approaches as well.

The question facing all educators today, as it has in the past, is whether our current educational system/structure/policies in the United States are able to meet the demands of a changing social and economic landscape.

As we examine U.S. education we increasingly criticize our capacity to be sufficiently strong ethically, politically, socially, and economically to secure a hope-filled future.

Educators who work in our nation's schools represent the conscience of a society because they shape the conditions under which future generations learn about themselves and their relationships to others in the world. Children learn not only through imitating adults but also through their schooling.

Educators, families, and community members need to reinvigorate the language, social relations, and politics of schooling. We must analyze how power shapes the direction of a school.

It has become a cliché to say that these are precarious times for public schools. It is also a reality. On the one hand, improving schools is the public's top priority. On the other, significant numbers of Americans are giving up on public schools. Today's parents and, indeed, all voters, need to see signs of success if they are to support public schools.

Winds of Change acknowledges that enormous problems *outside* schools do not mean that educators *inside* schools cannot do a better job at managing the school environment. The road to true equality is to give all students the gift of competition. I have designed this book to inform and assist those who wish to redefine problems so they can be solved.

My goal is to achieve results. Parents, teachers, policy makers, and students must come together to help make a difference. The national dialogue is beginning to change. *Winds of Change* can be a starting point.

This book grew out of my belief that racism, like all other forms of cruelty and tyranny, debases all human beings, those who are its victims, those who victimize, and in subtle ways those who are mere accessories.

Poverty also plays a huge part in our society. Poverty is not a neutral social factor. Associated with it are a variety of other social issues such as family instability, welfare dependency, crime, housing, unemployment, and low academic achievement.

Structural organization of society also plays a profound role in shaping the life chances of individuals. Opportunities, resources, and benefits are not distributed equally across the urban landscape. Some residential areas have more prestige, greater affluence, higher home values, better services, and safer streets than others. We must level the playing field and then get out there and play.

I write this book to support change, to help us understand ourselves, our students, and even our educational system. I have done nothing less than call it like I see it.

Diversity can only increase our knowledge, our joy, and can only add quality to our lives. However, we must be willing to talk and not avoid discussion. Then we must respond.

We must address issues of race, poverty, institutional responsibility, school culture, standardized testing, English language learners, and school violence. These issues become entwined with trends and results.

We must also allow for friction, edginess, dissention, and discomfort to enter into our schools. At the same time parents, colleagues, policy makers, neighbors, and students should be encouraged to come together despite our differences and because of our similarities.

I believe that educators too often want solutions to be quick and easy. They want something that will solve the problem now. Solutions will only happen when patterns change regarding unemployment, poverty, and economic equity. Change will happen when compassion and politics are no longer considered opposites.

In thinking about all these things, and in writing *Winds of Change*, I realize we are each on our own journey to understanding change.

We are the future. It is time to stand up. Together we have the power to transform the American education system.

Acknowledgments

Thank you, Marty, for loving me. I've become a better person because of you.

Thank you, Quintin Pettigrew. I would have given up on me, but you never did.

Thank you, Bob Brown. I am a teacher and administrator because of you, and the example and support you gave me. I am honored to be your friend.

Thank you, Judy Schulze and Jane Deeming, for showing me that teaching and integrity are inseparable.

Thank you, Tom Koerner, for taking an interest in my writing and giving me the courage to reach for the stars. I'll always be grateful.

Thank you, Ruby P., Lost Cauz, and Britt, my incredible students. When I was on the edge, your love and friendship pulled me back.

Thank you, Mona. You stood up for me when no one else would and it changed my life.

Introduction

Education: Reading, Writing, and Futility

> To each of us at certain points in our lives, there come opportunities to rearrange our formulas and assumptions. Not necessarily to be rid of the old, but more to profit from adding something new. —Leo Buscaglia

Those of us with kids (whether on the lawn or on the horizon) have a vested interest in education. In fact, next to parenting, education is the largest part of the foundation upon which a child will build his or her life. Shortchange them early on and they'll be paying the price for years (getting pregnant at sixteen or seventeen, taking on an absurd mortgage at twenty-five, tacking on an fifty extra pounds by thirty-five, etc.).

Parenting is up to us. We raise our sons and daughters the way we think they should be raised. We instill our values and we try to provide security and a nurturing environment. We cross our fingers and hope we're doing the right thing.

But education is different. For most of us parents, it's out of our hands. When the time comes, we usher our kids out from under our wings and shoo them on a bus.

We think of them learning to conjugate verbs, use correct pronouns, and assemble decent-sized sentences. We have faith that they'll be able to spell "Wednesday" without looking it up and give the name of the continent we live on without having to mull it over. We hope our children will be able to locate the state of Florida on a map, divide nine by three and know which countries made up the Axis and Allies in World War II. We want these things for our children because we know that learning history, science, math, and geography can help them succeed. We want to help them realize that education is the key to success.

In reality, with a few exceptions, our public schools are costly disasters (we throw four times more money at public schools than we did forty years ago) based on an antiquated tenure system and unmotivated teachers using overstuffed classrooms inside decaying buildings to pass on much of what they don't know to their undisciplined, uninterested students. These students then enter the workforce or college with a sub-par education that is slowly but steadily costing America her standing in the world.

Nationwide, over a million college students require remedial courses just to catch up. We are spending up to $2.5 billion a year to teach these kids what our billions in tax dollars should have already taught them.

In a recent poll conducted by National Geographic (2010), 63 percent of eighteen- to twenty-four-year-olds could not locate Iraq on a map, 70 percent shrugged their shoulders when asked where Iran and Israel were located, and 90 percent had no clue where Afghanistan was. On top of that, 50 percent could not even locate the state of New York.

Americans don't seem to agree on much anymore. But we do agree that education is in need of change.

Is education a federal issue? For more than two hundred years it was a local and state issue. Then along came Jimmy Carter who won approval to create the U.S. Department of Education. Control went from local and state governments to Washington, D.C. By the time George W. Bush signed the No Child Left Behind Act most Americans were completely anesthetized to the idea of national politicians being in charge of their kids' education. A single entity has the power to determine what our children learn and by what methods they learn it.

Education is about learning. Remember that! Along with government control came the progressive education movement. Progressives believe the educational environment should be nurturing and comforting. Using red pens to correct tests is out (red is harsh) and purple (soothing) is in.

Progressives attempt to "level the playing field" which many educators think translates to "lowering the standards." It's not fair to *judge* a child's work because there are no wrong answers, only life experiences.

Progressive education began with the goal of providing a nurturing environment that aimed at kids' hearts rather than their heads. The movement's leader, John Dewey, was a champion of educational reform and saw the teacher as more of a coach and did not agree with the concept that teachers teach students facts. That was so nineteenth century.

Teachers are not there to tell a child if he or she is "right or wrong," they are there to help the child through a touchy-feely period of self-awareness and discovery. Empathy over narrative was emphasized. Competition was viewed as unhealthy and grades were hurtful. Freedom was valued over structure.

Is progressive education a misplaced ideology that has let down generations of children?

Schools now enjoy four times more dollars per student than they did in the 1960s. Have schools gotten four times better? Have math and reading skills improved? Have graduation rates improved? No, they have not. Do you really think throwing more money at the problem will improve all of that?

It is worth mentioning that our Constitution makes absolutely no reference to schools or education because the federal government was never supposed to be in the education business in the first place. The Tenth Amendment—the powers not delegated to the United States by the Constitution . . . are reserved to the states respectively, or to the people—makes that pretty clear.

So what is the solution? How about school choice? If a parent doesn't want his or her child to go to a school, it's usually because the school is bad or dangerous. Do you blame the parent for wanting a better education for his or her child? In "normal" life we patronize businesses we like and we avoid those we don't. Should it be any different for schools?

School choice changes the whole equation. Under the voucher system tax dollars are attached to your child and the child becomes valuable to a school of your choice. With vouchers, the tax dollars you're coughing up can be spent on a school you're actually excited about. What a novel idea!

When parents are given the option to move their kids from traditional public schools to charter schools, they line up in droves. Why? Because they know charter schools have accountability for their results.

Take the Thurgood Marshall Academy (TMA) charter school located in Washington, D.C.'s Ward 8. This area is home to 30 percent of all the city's homicides, has the lowest average income in the city ($14,000 per year) and has the lowest graduation rates in a city full of low graduation rates.

However, Thurgood Marshall Academy is an oasis. Despite everything working against them, students there have managed to post 95 percent attendance rates along with the third highest test scores of any D.C. school. Every single graduate goes on to college.

This is reason enough to support school choice. Schools should not be monopolies. They should compete for dollars with other schools. They should strive to earn your business and attract students with incentives like having better teachers, more curricular options, and more high-tech classrooms. Competition is good!

Schools face a relentless torrent of demands without receiving the kinds of support they need and deserve. Schools have the responsibility today of educating not only their own school community, but also the larger community, about value, relevance, and requirements of a student-centered education.

The art of good teaching is complex. A lack of understanding of this complexity leads to many simplistic policy prescriptions: test driven accountability, "magic" teacher-proof curriculum, merit pay, paying students for performance, and running schools like businesses. The proponents of these popular fixes for schools largely share the common characteristic of being noneducators. None of these reforms address the nature of teaching and learning, nor do they reflect the growing support among educators for personalization, real-world learning, and performance-based assessment.

One of the beauties of intergenerational learning is that it honors the achievements and wisdom of people who don't make it into the history books.

Educators on the front lines have a hundred criticisms of our school system and the list grows daily. The hope is that we can improve our system, since public education in a vibrant, dynamic democracy should never be considered finished. But the reform should be based on facts about the system and input from its practitioners. Reforms proposed by politicians, business leaders, or other citizens should not be undertaken without reliable evidence or credible stories of experience to back them up.

Many educators were concerned that so much nonsense could be spoken and written in the United States about the glories of the Japanese educational system that perhaps information about the American system could also be false. We must begin, therefore, to examine the validity of the criticisms made about our educational system.

We need to look closely at some of the commonly repeated charges made against the American public school system. But this time, instead of simply arguing with critics, because they appeal to our suspicions and fears, let us ask whether any credible data exist. Perhaps the charges will turn out to be only partially true. Perhaps our public education is failing certain students and their families and not others, and perhaps it is not even failing most of the students in our public schools.

Perhaps Americans have been lied to, because when nations have economic difficulties or go through social change, their leaders look for scapegoats, and the American school system is a handy one. Perhaps we are changing into a plutocracy, where a wealthy elite chooses not to use the public schools and participates in undermining confidence in that system so as to promote the conception of schooling as a commodity, to be bought like medicine, to be regarded as a privilege rather than a right of every American. Perhaps we are in a peculiarly American cycle, where every generation or so we like to play "kick the teacher."

We must look again at the reasons underlying the changes made and the need for change.

Educators tend to agree that, touted as an unsinkable ship of social progress for more than a century, public schooling is leaking badly. Achievement is stagnant or declining, public opinion is low, and community conflict over what is taught seems to be ever increasing. Some schools, especially in the inner city, have already slid beneath the waves, extinguishing the hopes and dreams of countless children. Literally thousands of would-be reformers have suggested patches here and there, but water just keeps flooding in.

If the education of the next generation is not to be completely forsaken, we need to cast aside our assumptions about how schools should be run, and consider not only major overhauls to the current system, but entirely different approaches as well. This is not an easy task.

We first have to understand people's educational needs before we can determine which sorts of school systems most effectively serve those needs.

It is clear that there is a fundamental kernel of agreement among parents on the importance of basic academic subjects. People expect that, at a minimum, their children will have mastered reading, writing, and demonstrated math concepts by the time they are out of high school. There is an equally strong emphasis on career preparation, since parents from Milwaukee to Munich consider landing a good job to be one of the main purposes of education. Beyond these basics, priorities diverge, wildly.

Whenever a state-run school system adopts one set of priorities at the expense of all others, conflict inevitably ensues. Consider the battle over religion in classrooms that has plagued the United States for more than one hundred years, and the rest of the world centuries before that.

Clearly we need a system that can cater to differences between families, but what about people without school-age children? To the extent that the general public subsidizes education by whatever means, it can rightly ask that its needs be met as well. Fortunately parents and nonparents agree that basic academics and career preparation are keys to student success. Most people consider any contributions that education can make to the harmony of social and economic relations as desirable. Finally citizens expect to get their money's worth from the schools. If costs increase, student achievement should go up as well.

That said, we can now ask: Does public education have what it takes? There is little question that it is mainly there to fulfill the goals outlined above. So the question really becomes: Can public education be fixed; or should we cut our losses and replace it with something fundamentally different?

Reformers have suggested a whole range of strategies for improving our schools, from new curriculum and tougher standards, to charter schools, vouchers, and even complete privatization.

To know which are really likely to succeed and which aren't, we need to identify reasons why public education does not seem to be working in the first place. The most promising way of answering that question is to compare school systems around the world, starting with ancient times and working forward all the way to the present. By doing so, we can discover what has worked, what hasn't, and why.

What history shows us is that the problems of high spending, lack of successful innovation, unresponsiveness to the needs of families, and social strife over what is taught are mainly caused by the way public schools are run, not by the people who staff them or the particular standards or curriculum they adopt.

Educators argue that it is the absence of competition between schools that stifles innovation, the lack of potential profits that makes applied educational research and development a waste of money, and the lack of parental freedom of choice that sets family against family in a bitter fight for ideological control of the schools.

These are conclusions that few people want to hear, much less believe. Public education has a long history in most industrial countries, and we have all grown accustomed to it. But however much we may want public schools to work, there is insurmountable evidence that it has never worked as well as competitive educational markets.

We can have the educational outcomes we want (higher academic achievement, effective innovation, social harmony on school issues, responsive teachers, reasonable costs, etc.) but we may have to give up the cherished but false notion that they can be provided by government. The government is only one of many tools.

It is hoped that we can open our minds and realize that choice will help citizens to assess the relative merits of public education and free education markets, and make the best decision for the future of their children and communities.

We are seeing today, amid government turmoil throughout the world, the market leading us into a double-dip recession and unemployment, and also the lack of leadership that means public education in the United States does not fulfill either the educational or social needs of children. Its deficiencies have serious negative consequences in our political system, our economy, and within our social and cultural affairs.

We need to listen to the voices seeking to improve education. One group in particular, the Educational Policy Institute in Washington, D.C., seeks to improve education through research, policy analysis, and the development of responsible alternatives to existing policies and practices. In addition, the

Institute strives to promote parental choices in education, a competitive education industry, and other policies that address the problems of both public and private schools.

"People must have freedom of mind for research that makes progress, otherwise there is no use in having an educational system. If everyone remained in the same groove and were taught exactly the same thing, we would end up with a nation of mediocrities." Former president Harry Truman sounded this warning in 1956. When will we listen?

Has the public educational system in the United States served this nation well? Today and in the future it will meet unprecedented challenges.

The time is right to assess the strengths and weaknesses of the American public educational system. We need to build on its strengths and shore up its weaknesses. We know more than ever about how to do this. However, serious questions remain about the resources we are willing to devote to the task and about our political will to get the job done.

Winds of Change will give you some answers. This book addresses why some schools are failing, our changing demographics and English-language learners, dangerous schools and violence, poverty, testing, who influences education in America, new trends, and future trends.

Writers about educational reform and change are aware that a single text does not have the power to do all things. A text not honestly and passionately written can do nothing. This book is an honest attempt to look at the Winds of Change that have brought education to where we stand today.

POINTS TO REMEMBER

- Education is in need of change. School choice may be the answer.
- The U.S. Constitution makes no reference to schools or education.
- Reforms proposed by politicians, business leaders, and other citizens should not be undertaken without reliable evidence or credible stories of experience to back them up.
- We have to understand people's educational needs before we can determine which sorts of school systems most effectively serve those needs.
- The absence of competition between schools stifles innovation.
- We need to listen to the voices seeking to improve education.

Chapter One

Are Public Schools Hazardous to Our Health? Heated Rhetoric and Force of Habit Inhibit Change

Take a method and try it, if it fails admit it frankly, and try another. But by all means try something. —Franklin D. Roosevelt

For a diverse nation, we share a remarkable consensus with respect to educating children. As reflected in polls and focus groups, Americans are nearly unanimous in their commitment to certain fundamental ideals: that all children have access to a quality education, regardless of family income; that they be taught the rights and duties of citizenship; and that the schools help to foster strong and cohesive communities. These are the ideals of public education.

One hundred and fifty years ago, a band of dedicated reformers declared that progress toward those ideals was too slow and proposed that a new institution be created to more effectively promote them. Led by Bostonian Horace Mann, the reformers campaigned for a greater state role in education.

They argued that a universal, centrally planned system of tax funded schools would be superior in every respect to the seemingly disorganized market of independent schools that existed at the time. Shifting the reins of educational power from private to public hands, they promised, would yield better teaching methods and materials, greater efficiency, superior service to the poor, and a stronger more cohesive nation. Mann even ventured the prediction that if public schooling were widely adopted and given enough time to work, nine-tenths of the crimes in the penal code would become obsolete.

Though Horace Mann's promised nirvana has clearly failed to material-ize, there is one respect in which he and his fellow reformers were complete-ly successful. They forged an unbreakable link in people's minds between the institution of public schooling and the ideals of public education.

As generation after generation has attended public schools and sent its children to public schools, it has become more and more difficult to see the distinction between the institution itself and the principles it is meant to uphold. (If you believe in our shared ideals of public education, then you must support the public schools.)

This seemingly innocuous failure to distinguish between means and ends has had two disastrous consequences. First, it has meant that any criticism of the public school system could be, and often has been, misconstrued as an attack on the ideals of public education. As a result, individuals who agree on the ultimate goals of education, but who differ as to the most effective way of achieving those goals are repeatedly and unnecessarily thrown into conflict. Where cooperation and mutual respect could flourish, endless bickering and antagonism are the norm.

The second consequence has been an extreme narrowing of vision. Schol-ars and policy makers who have equated public education solely with public schooling have contented themselves with reform efforts that merely tinker around the edges of our current system. They have consistently failed to consider the vast wealth of evidence that exists on alternative approaches to education, thereby reducing their chances of identifying the most effective practices.

We have suffered with the weight of these consequences far too long. Despite decades of heroic efforts to improve public schools, the institution continues to fall short of our expectations. Over the past fifty years, we have cut the pupil-teacher ratio in half, quadrupled the per-student spending, and tested innumerable reform programs. In desperation, we have ascribed the blame for the system's ills to every level of public school employee from teachers and principals to administrators and superintendents. Nevertheless, the ills persist.

The most fundamental skill of all, literacy, has actually been in decline in this country for at least thirty years. According to the most sophisticated national and international literacy studies, nearly a quarter of American six-teen- to twenty-five-year-olds have only the most meager grasp of reading and writing.

Pedagogical methods and teacher training, which were promised to make great strides under the guidance of government experts, have languished. Some instructional techniques have been sidelined by the public schools for decades despite their proven effectiveness. And most poignantly, the public schools have failed to fulfill one of our most important and universally held ideals of public education: providing a decent education to all low-income children.

We cannot afford to continue squandering our time and our children's futures on heated rhetoric and unthinking devotion to the status quo. While public schooling has become deeply entrenched in our nation's tradition, we must realize that it is only one among many possible approaches to education. We must not let the force of habit stand in the way of our ultimate aims. Instead, we must consider a broad range of school systems to determine which is best suited to advancing those aims.

Since most developed nations adopted state-run school systems during the nineteenth century, it might not be immediately obvious where to find examples of alternative approaches to schooling. The answer has been right behind us all along the 2,500-year history of education. Our ancestors tried so many different ways of educating their children, more ways than most people would imagine, yet we continue to ignore their experiences at our society's peril.

While it doesn't make sense to point to any one historical education system and try to copy it (there are a number of factors that would cause a system to work well in one culture and not in another), it does make sense to compare educational approaches from a variety of times and places and to identify common elements of the most successful systems. Any approach to schooling that consistently produced good results across many different cultures, regardless of the prevailing social, political, and economic conditions might have some interesting lessons to teach us.

Studies have been made comparing school systems all over the world (Andrew Coulson, 2009), from ancient times to the present, in an attempt to discover which systems met the needs of citizens, which did not, and why.

From classical Greece through the medieval Islamic empire, from the young American republic up to the present, a recurrent theme emerged from the hum of the centuries: competitive educational markets have consistently done a better job of serving the public than state-run educational systems.

The reason lies in the fact that state school systems lack four key factors that history tells us are essential to educational excellence: choice and financial responsibility for parents, and freedom and market incentives for educators. School systems that have enjoyed these characteristics have consistently done the best job of meeting both our private educational demands and our shared educational ideals.

Though it is widely thought that government intervention was necessary to bring schooling and literacy to the masses, both England and the United States achieved those milestones before state-run educational systems were firmly established in either nation. It is also ironic that, while one of the chief aims of public education was to foster peaceful, harmonious communities, public schools have actually caused great divisiveness.

Because public schools constitute the official government organ of education, everyone wants them to reflect their own views. In a pluralistic society that is impossible. When one group forces its views on the public schools, it does so at the expense of all others, creating inevitable turmoil.

Battles over such things as evolution versus creation, book selection and censorship, and sex education are endemic to state-run schooling. Free market school systems, by contrast, have allowed people to pursue both their own unique educational needs and their shared educational goals without coming into conflict with each other.

One of the great promises of public schools was that they would end social inequities, providing a quality education to all students regardless of income. Today, market-oriented educational reforms such as vouchers and tuition tax credits are often opposed on the grounds that they would break that promise. However, those who worry about low-income families falling through the cracks in an education market cannot ignore the reality that the public school system is currently dumping countless children into a yawning educational chasm.

The bulk of evidence, both historical and modern, points to the superiority of markets (supplemented with a mechanism for subsidizing the education of low-income children) over state school systems in their ability to serve the poor.

Throughout history low-income parents have consistently made better educational decisions for their own children than government experts have made for them, no matter how well-intentioned those experts have been. Poor parents, indeed all parents, need to be empowered to once again take control of their children's education.

To many, the concept of an open market for education will seem preposterous. After all, we have been led to believe that education is different, that it does not benefit from market forces in the way that other enterprises do. In light of the historical evidence, we have clearly been misled.

While most fields of human endeavor have seen astonishing growth and improvement over the course of the past century, while whole new industries have been created and general intelligence has steadily increased, educational achievement alone has stagnated, a fossilized legacy of central planning and good intentions gone awry.

If the lessons of history can be distilled to a single observation, it may be that the institution of public schooling, as it is today, is not the best system for advancing our ideals of public education. After 150 years of experimentation and decades of disappointment, is it not time that we consider alternatives to the public school system?

As alternative environments are implemented, policy makers are encouraged to assess the impact of alternative programs on the rest of the system, and to consider their political role in broader school reform.

Alternative education is a perspective, not a procedure or program. It is based on the belief that there are many ways to become educated, as well as many types of environments and structures within which this may occur. It recognizes that all people can be educated and that it is in society's interest to ensure that all are educated to a general high school level. To accomplish this requires that we provide a variety of structures and environments so each person can make progress.

The primary goal is to help young people become productive members of society. A large part of the responsibility for achieving this goal is assigned to the school system. It is suggested that schools meet students' differing needs rather than expect them to conform to one particular educational environment. A long history of initiatives for students facing challenging situations is evidence of the belief in helping *all* students succeed.

A second goal also drives the establishment of alternative programs: the need to remove disruptive influences to create classrooms that are productive and safe. Many educators and policymakers recognize this need, but disapprove of discipline policies and simply remove students from school, leaving them with no adult guidance or supervision.

We are therefore left with several issues. Do alternative programs really work? Which programs work best? Are there consequences for the rest of the educational system?

Proponents of alternative education claim that it dramatically improves the academic achievement and behavior of dropouts and potential dropouts. Research echoes this. Students in alternative programs report both satisfaction with their education and confidence that the program will meet their needs.

The most easily recognized aspects of a successful program include such features as culture, climate, curriculum, instructional links to other programs, and social services. Successful programs vary in their specific features because program creators design each to meet the needs of a unique student population. These programs focus on the whole student, relationships, expanded teacher roles, sense of community, and higher student expectations. The organizational structure includes relative autonomy, comprehensive programs, counseling, safe environment, academic innovation, and school-linked services.

We also know that not all students should be in alternative programs. However, we do need to focus on those students who are at-risk in traditional classrooms, where they are underserved. In addition, another group to keep in mind are the quiet, underachieving students that we tend to forget.

We need to explore not only how alternative programs lead to success but also how they fit into the educational system as a whole.

Confronting the failures of the traditional system may be more successful if we address the root causes of student learning problems and create more flexible teaching and learning environments. Such changes may diminish negative outcomes, allowing more students to succeed. A keener focus on restructuring the educational system could make alternative environments more acceptable.

Educators need to ask themselves whether they want to help students who are failing and then take a first step toward improving schools for everyone. Consider which program is the most successful and move forward from there.

We need a jump-start to accelerate learning. In most urban schools less than 50 percent of students of color were proficient in reading and less than 35 percent were passing statewide reading tests. These schools fail to make adequate yearly progress and often end up on the state and federal watch list of poorly performing schools.

School reformers continue to call for a more intense focus on reading and math. That means "weeding the garden" or getting rid of present practices that stand in the way of progress.

Enter the "90-90-90" programs. This stands for 90 percent low income, 90 percent students of color, and 90 percent of the students achieving at high academic levels. These programs have a fierce focus on a select few academic areas, frequent student assessment, an emphasis on nonfiction writing, and teachers who team together to evaluate student work. Using these strategies, Norfolk, Virginia's, and Boston, Massachusetts's, schools have made significant, sustained academic student gains.

The underlying theme is that students must make progress quickly in order to break the cycle of underachievement being passed on from generation to generation. This new approach won't work unless the teachers get the support they need to shift gears. Without it, classroom educators can easily dismiss the idea as just another short-lived fad that will change with the turnover in school leadership.

The term "90-90-90" was originally coined by Douglas Reeves in 1995 based on observations he made in Milwaukee, Wisconsin. Since that time the term has been broadly applied to describe successful academic performance in schools with significant numbers of poor and minority students.

Students write frequently in a variety of subjects. Performance assessment in several disciplines is used. Teachers collaborate using authentic student work as the focus of their discussions. In addition schools make dramatic changes in their schedules. They change goals and strategies mid-term if needed. They even move teachers around based on their teaching ability and subject knowledge.

The emphasis is always on student achievement, and those who are unable to meet the high standards are placed in an intervention program. Students are never failures. Some simply need more time to reach their level of success. Student learning is the goal, not the grading. Multiple school assessment practices are implemented. There is a place for standardized assessment, teacher-developed assessment, and performance assessment along with other ways of finding the students' level of achievement. The sad thing is that few schools are even looking at this program.

Let's focus on high schools for a moment.

The vast majority of the nation's public high schools were designed for another time, and today they are far out of sync with the demands of our diverse republic and a global economy. Are our high schools obsolete?

Many educators feel we need to redesign our high schools into diverse schools. The diversity of these schools is one of their most encouraging features. We need to transcend the battle lines set by liberals who fight with conservatives over reform strategies and the progressives who clash with traditionalists over ideological and partisan enterprise in America.

We need a choice system that permits students and parents to select schools and thus encourage schools to be different. The large, traditional comprehensive high schools no longer work. Not only do students in the inner city drop out but also those in middle-class suburbs, rural areas, and everywhere in between.

New schools are important for underserved students, increasing their options, reducing enrollments in overcrowded schools, and leveraging change in other existing schools through competition for students.

We must salute and support those who are leading the fight, teachers who never give up on students, principals who hold fast to their vision of a great school for low-income students, superintendents who build a sense of community, educational entrepreneurs, community organizers fighting for families, university deans who roll up their sleeves in schools, mayors with visions of great cities, and governors who know that education equals jobs.

We also should salute the students, especially those who grow up in America in poverty, and those who come to this country for a better life, who in the face of great odds persevere to gain an education.

The nation has entered a new era. New demands mean change. Sorting students into curriculum tracks worked in an industrial era where the majority of the jobs required workers to use their hands rather than their heads and paid them well for doing this. But in today's knowledge-based economy, where decent paying jobs require brains rather than brawn, only students who are taught to use their minds will have a chance at a middle-class lifestyle or more.

Modern democratic life also demands more. Effective citizenship in today's complex world requires a level of knowledge about science, global politics, and a host of other subjects, that in the past only a small elite possessed.

Alienated educators still believe that students are incapable of doing demanding academic work. By believing this educators absolve themselves of the responsibility of teaching challenging subjects. It is easier to teach basic math and general science than to teach trigonometry, calculus, physics, or chemistry.

High schools of three or four thousand students make matters worse. Big schools are bureaucratic places. Roles and relationships are defined by rules and regulations. For African American and Hispanic students these schools are dead ends.

Why doesn't the public listen? Since 1980, respected reformers such as Ernest Boyer (Carnegie Foundation), John Goodlad (University of Washington), and Theodore Sizer (Dean of Harvard Grad School of Education) came to much the same conclusion and urged a reshaping of secondary education. Their reports spawned an immense amount of school reform but unfortunately secondary schools were pushed aside in favor of other priorities.

Then in 2000, the Bill and Melinda Gates Foundation launched a five-year initiative to replace comprehensive high schools with a very different institution, one designed to educate many more students to a much higher level as today's economy demands.

The foundation discovered, as Boyer, Sizer, Goodlad, and others before them did, that high schools must be small, personalized, and individualized. Smaller schools encourage stronger bonds between students and teachers and generate a level of genuine caring and mutual obligation.

Students and teachers work harder on each other's behalf. Students are prepared for postsecondary success. Students' minds are stretched, projects and presentations abound. Students become active learners, inquiring, questioning, independent-minded individuals, and not passive receptacles of received wisdom.

The bottom line is that we must educate students and educate them well. Hugging is not the same as algebra. Rigor and loving care must be braided together or we run the risk of creating small, nurturing environments that aren't schools. Keeping students connected to schools and learning is critical, but ultimately, it's merely a means to a larger end—student achievement.

There are changes that must be made to the status quo. These changes will be worth the hard work needed to achieve them. Changes must happen if we are to narrow the test score gaps between racially ethnic groups and white students.

The Obama administration tried to assist educators in closing the gaps by creating a program called "Race to the Top," which created competition among states to provoke serious improvement in public school systems. Teacher evaluations were to be tied to student achievement. Pay higher salaries for performance, not seniority. Place teachers in schools that need them and find more ways to take advantage of what excellent teachers bring to the table.

Administrators need to be held accountable for district performance. We must do whatever it takes to help students at under-performing schools succeed and be prepared for life after high school. Many districts are getting rid of their principals. In other districts policymakers are looking at what is going on first, and then deciding what the plan should be. In some cases changing the principal may not be what is best for the students.

Educators need to find a way to revamp our postsecondary teacher preparation programs. Many educators are describing our public school system as a relic. Maybe one of our biggest challenges is complacency.

President Obama says that the Race to the Top competition is a means to an end, an incentive to do what we ought to do anyway. States need to project an image of innovation and above average performance for our school-age children. We can no longer sit around and admire our reflection. The competition is getting smarter and bolder. Education will make or break our nation.

When all is said and done, achievement matters! There is a crisis in our classrooms. In virtually every school district across America, African American children achieve at lower levels and have even worse test scores, are placed more frequently into special education classrooms or remedial and less challenging classes, are discouraged from striving to excel academically or demanding excellence from themselves.

The perception is that they are intellectually inferior. This is tragically reinforced by a vocal and destructive segment within our own culture that seeks to portray academic achievement as a sellout to a "white" society. We cannot allow those attitudes to continue. Indifference toward academic achievement will doom our children to a future far beneath their capabilities. This has to stop!

We must reject the self-destructive mindset that teaches our children to accept academic mediocrity. We must instill a lifelong enthusiasm for education as a reward in itself. Remember the Urban League slogan: Our Children = Our Destiny!

We have a right to demand and get good schools. Parents shoulder a huge responsibility with the schools to make sure a child learns and achieves. Jobs today are skilled or professional positions. Young people without much education have little prayer of qualifying for these jobs.

Good schools today devote more time to reading and math instruction. Students need to be monitored closely and interventions offered quickly if the student falters.

The sorry fact, though, is that all too many inner city and rural schools that serve low-income children and students of color leave much to be desired. The teachers are overwhelmed and students are performing below par and way below their potential. Things must be shaken up for the sake of the children. Parents and community leaders should do the shaking until educators and boards of education get the message.

It is not hard to go about pressuring politicians and educators to improve schools. First, insist on no-nonsense leadership. Change requires risk and risk taking requires risk takers. Second, demand accountability, which is a two-way street. It begins with adults who run the schools and the parents who rear the children. It ends with the children themselves who will either enjoy the benefits of solid academic preparation or else pay the ultimate price of failure.

Third, professionalize the teaching profession. Without good teachers, there won't be good schools. It is as simple as that! Fourth, provide challenging courses for *all* children. Students, poor and rich alike, learn to high levels when they are taught to high levels. However, low-income students and children of color in this country are systematically bludgeoned into low academic performance with a steady dose of low level, boring, if not downright silly assignments and curricula. Stop sorting our kids into bins of winners and losers.

Parents and teachers need to be vigilant, informed, involved, and visible, and they need to organize others who will advocate for change.

It is said Masai warriors in Africa greet one another with the words: "Eserian Nakera." The lyrical phrase means: "And how are the children?" The traditional response is: "All the children are well." The transformation of American public education will be complete when the schools embrace that Masai saying, in word and in deed.

The skills that each of us needs throughout our careers as well as our lives as husbands, wives, parents, and citizens of the United States and the world are these: literacy, mathematics, reasoning and critical thinking, science, citizenship, and computer literacy. Every child should emerge from the American educational system with these six skills well in hand. The child must be told over and over again, and understand, that he or she is worthy.

Adults know there are no guarantees in life. But we also know from hard-earned experience that academic achievement gives young people the best possible shot at becoming victors instead of victims.

You've probably also heard the old saying, "It takes an entire village to raise a child." This saying is just flowery rhetoric unless we make it real. It is our collective duty to make certain our children get the high quality education they need and deserve. Then we, the villagers of America, can rightfully say: "All the children are well."

POINTS TO REMEMBER

- Literacy has been in decline for more than thirty years.
- Public schooling is only one among many possible approaches to education.
- Alternative education is a perspective, not a procedure or program.
- Large high schools are bureaucratic places.
- Achievement matters!
- Change requires risk, accountability is a two-way street, and providing challenging courses for all children are some of the answers for informed citizens.

Chapter Two

School Culture

Whatever it Takes

In memory of those brilliant young souls for whom it might have been different, and on behalf of so many today for whom it still can be. —Rachael
Kessler

It was April 14, 2004, a cool, wet night in Harlem. The hand-lettered sign out
front of PS242, streaked with raindrops, said, "Welcome to the Promise
Academy Charter School."

Geoffrey Canada, a tall, thin, black man in a dark blue suit, surveyed the
crowd. From what he could see, the parents taking their seats were the ones
he had hoped to attract: typical Harlem residents, mostly African American,
some Hispanic, almost all poor or working class, all struggling to one degree
or another with the challenges of raising and educating children in one of
New York City's most impoverished neighborhoods.

Canada had embarked on an outsized and audacious new endeavor; a
poverty-fighting project that was different from anything that had come before it. Canada realized it was not the outcome of individual programs that he
really cared about. What mattered was the overall impact he wanted to have
on the children he was trying to serve. He was all too familiar with the "fade-
out" phenomenon, where a group of needy kids are helped along by one
program or another, only to return to the disappointing mean soon after the
program ends.

Head Start, the government-funded pre-kindergarten program for low-
income children was the classic example. Studies showed that graduates of
Head Start entered kindergarten ahead of their inner-city peers. Studies years
later showed that some students had slipped back to the anemic achievement

13

level of neighborhood kids who had not attended Head Start. A few years of bad school culture and bad surroundings were powerful enough to wipe out all of the program's gains.

We need to find a way off the treadmill. Who do we want to help? What is our goal for them? What do you need to accomplish that?

Students need to survive adolescence, graduate from high school, go on to college, and graduate from college into life. Inner city youth must learn to resist negative forces in their community that have the potential to destroy their lives. It is very difficult for many of them to make it through what is referred to as the "four critical years": those after middle school and before college.

These years are the students' Bermuda Triangle. Those who manage to steer clear of the dangers of these four years wind up with a stronger sense of who they are. Many who successfully navigate the years from middle school to college attribute their success to self-determination, strength, and an ability to maintain focus on their future. Our school culture must nurture these qualities.

The achievement gap between students of color and white students was first noted fifty years ago. At that time the family background was said to be the cause. Since then, other explanations, including peer groups, culture, discrimination, heredity, and schooling have been offered.

We now know more about what the causes and consequences of the achievement gap are than how to close it. We have tried several remedies: reducing class size, providing options to attend private schools through vouchers, high stakes accountability, and reform after reform.

Four major barriers stand in our way. First, no clear strategy has emerged on how to achieve this goal. Second, no clear definition of what this gap is has come into play. Third, educators disagree on how to provide effective academic instruction. Fourth, educators and policy makers have ignored curriculum orientation and other factors that some schools find successful.

Teachers must understand a student's life experiences and how one responds to them. Teachers need to integrate knowledge from several fields—education, sociology, anthropology, and social work, to name a few—in their instruction.

The turmoil that students of color experience is deeply rooted in the history of America. You have three stages for black students: their ancestral past in Africa, the coming of the slave ships and the system of slavery that arose in America, and the period after the Civil War.

In Africa boys were able to develop a sense of personal power and shared values, which led to self-identity and masculinity. Then came psychological and spiritual shock as they were shipped from Africa in chains into slavery in America. Once in America these uprooted African men experienced no legal rights and were forced to live according to a Euro-American worldview, which differed dramatically from the one that had shaped their lives. After years of conditioning such men came to believe they were inferior human beings.

Black male inferiority was reinforced in the post-Civil War period. American society cemented black males into a subservient role. Stereotypes of the black male as subhuman, unintelligent, sexually promiscuous, the idle buffoon, were everywhere, in stage shows, in novels, advertisements, and newspapers and magazines.

Social barriers were created, and lynching and Jim Crow laws were set in place. Educational, economic, political, and social disenfranchisement made it impossible for African Americans to climb above the bottom rung of the social ladder in education, jobs, income, and political power. This historical context contributed to turmoil.

Several present-day factors contribute to the turmoil all people of color experience in society today: globalization, urban economics, neglect, mass media, public policy regarding criminal justice, persistent racial discrimination, crumbling community infrastructures, and the lack of fulfillment of the civil rights promises.

Today, students of color are growing up in an era of globalization that has adversely affected their communities by contributing to urban economic neglect as job opportunities become scarce. Unemployment rates are rising. There has been an overall decline in the quality of life for urban youth, which has ushered in higher levels of drug-related crime and violence. The promises of the civil rights era have not materialized, thus causing students to believe that the American dream and the prosperity reflected in the media are unattainable.

Movies from the 1990s, such as *Juice, Menace II Society, New Jack City*, and *Belly*, present blacks as out of control, dangerous, and synonymous with drugs and violence.

The history of people of color and their present condition in America are generally overlooked when educators plan reforms. Perhaps this is a form of Racial America?

Responses to turmoil are influenced by the intensity of the turmoil that has been experienced. Multiple survival techniques have been developed including the "cool pose," a coping mechanism to hide self-doubt, insecurity, and inner turmoil. It can be observed in dress (beltless pants hanging well below the waist), manner of talk (rapping), and behavior (special handshakes).

Rap music also reflects a loss of hope and limited aspirations for the future. In one of his posthumous releases, Tupac Shakur, a slain, black, male rapper, sings, "The promise of a better tomorrow ain't never reached me because my teachers were too petrified to teach me." Shakur's suggested mistrust of his school environment and confusion about his place in the world is not unique. They are feelings shared by many urban youth on reaching adolescence.

The overall goal is to help teachers and administrators create a school culture with classrooms where inner city youth receive academic instruction that both promotes academic excellence and nurtures a positive identity of who they are and what they can become. Having this nurturing environment can combat the feelings of those who see schools as unwelcoming, hostile environments.

We, as educators and parents can help our youth develop strategies and hope for overcoming social and academic barriers. Such strategies will cause them to search for meaning in their lives and to challenge the status quo.

Before we can develop a school culture we need to step back and look at the meaning of culture. Educators believe culture consists of ever-changing values, traditions, social and political relationships, and worldview. It is shared and transformed by a group of people who are bound together by history, geographic location, language, social class, and religion.

How big of an impact does culture have on students' educational achievement? Very simply, students respond to schooling based on both their perception of the treatment they receive in school and their perception of what schooling can do for them in the future.

When relating culture to school, focus on day-to-day realities, relationships between home and school, student-teacher interaction patterns, teacher instructional practices, and assessment strategies. Considering culture in this way may reveal differences that need to be addressed. Therefore advocate for a culturally responsive approach to teaching. Meet the needs of the students. Reflect on your role. Understand yourself.

A pendulum swings both ways for students. On one side are hopes and dreams where potential can lead to promise. On the other is defeat where hopes unfulfilled become a record of human tragedy.

Educators talk a lot about school culture, but have we ever really looked at different schools and their culture? Testing is a school culture. Hey kids: Tests help you learn. Students who quiz themselves more often recall information more easily. Tests aren't just a way for teachers to torture their students. The brain encodes better mental hints during test taking than during studying alone. This study, published in the October 15, 2010, issue of the *Journal of Science*, suggests that rather than dread tests, students should embrace them.

Although many view tests as a way to mark and grade students' progress, research has found that the act of retrieving information from memory actually makes remembering it easier. The tests improve learning. This involves using concepts, ideas, or phrases that connect one piece of information to another. The more test practice you do, the better you become at knowing which concepts, ideas, or phrases to use.

Many charter schools have had good results by designing a program around testing. New York and Chicago are two cities that have started to close the testing gap. New Orleans is still dominated by charters and choice. Since 2007, the New Orleans schools have doubled the percentage of students scoring at basic competency levels or above.

The use of high stakes tests is changing what goes on in classrooms. Is this to the detriment of the arts, problem solving, creativity, and the joy of discovering? Hours are spent cramming the material covered on the tests to the neglect of subject areas like social studies, art, drama, and music. There is also an unwarranted stress placed on the students and teachers because of the intense pressure to raise scores. Many believe the continual drill and practice for tests leaves challenged learners even farther behind.

I would like to challenge states and districts to reexamine high stakes tests and their policies. Decisions have been made about grade promotion or graduation based on a single test, even if given multiple times. How about using course grades, validations, portfolios, and teacher judgment to determine who passes? Teachers know their students better than any test can. Consider a student's strengths and weaknesses, and capabilities. Entrust the decision making to the teachers. Allow them freedom to teach, plan, and develop engaging and innovative instruction.

Does a school culture of high stakes testing lead to cheating? School's out, but summer vacation 2011 is anything but relaxing for those embroiled in the most extensive cheating scandal in the history of American public education.

The summer of 2011 brought forth the results of a ten-month investigation in Georgia. It was revealed that pervasive tampering with standardized tests in Atlanta Public Schools had taken place. Teachers and administrators, not students are the culprits.

The report implicated 178 educators, including 38 principals at dozens of schools. American public education was to be the training ground of civic virtue. Instead, Atlanta students have gotten an object lesson in hypocrisy and corruption. The findings would be scandalous for anyone in a position of trust. They are especially so for public employees entrusted with children.

We expect teachers to set a good example. Instead some Atlanta teachers held "changing parties" to correct wrong answers on tests. In other cases, proctors provided extra time or even gave answers to students during testing.

Some supervisors apparently knew about the cheating, or even instigated the practices. A climate of intimidation pervaded the schools convincing teachers that their jobs were at risk if they didn't cooperate. Of course their jobs were also at risk if their students performed poorly on the tests.

In the background of this scandal is a policy increasing pressure on schools to make gains in standardized test scores. In 2002, the No Child Left Behind Act for the first time prescribed a federally driven testing regimen for local schools. It stipulated that all students be proficient in reading and math by 2014. The looming deadline may help explain, but should not be an excuse, for cheating. Producing data that feign progress is a dereliction of duty. Even worse, this cheating ring made a mockery of educations' highest purpose.

Aristotle said that education should teach a child to love what he ought to love. Schools should cultivate the virtues essential for self-government.

In American history, schools traditionally shaped the moral and intellectual life of the individual, drawing on a rich, classical, Christian heritage. Investing in individuals would lead to civilized society. By the early twentieth century, amid massive immigration to America, progressive education theory introduced social reform goals into the classroom. The goal became socialization by experts.

With cheating scandals also surfacing in Philadelphia, Los Angeles, Washington, D.C., and many other towns and cities across America, maybe public schools should have concentrated more on the moral lessons about honesty rather than socialization.

Today, "competitiveness" is the great policy pressure on schools. No Child Left Behind and other centralized, one-size-fits-all policies imply that this goal is too important to entrust to those closest to the students, their parents, teachers, and principals. So parents enjoy less leverage than do education unions and district bureaucrats. Centralized policy has made educators less responsive to meeting the needs of individual students and more attentive to making things look good on paper to comply with federal law.

To restore integrity in education, we ought to put greater authority in the hands of those with the greatest interest in the moral and intellectual formation of children, the parents.

Human history is littered with the wreckage of utopian visions that sought social progress through central action. The paradox of the American educational experiment is that cultivating individual moral responsibility and trusting individuals with self-government is the best way to ensure the common good.

Let's look at a school culture without No Child Left Behind. Students of color and poor kids have not made desired gains. Nearly a decade after Congress enacted NCLB, a sweeping mandate to ramp up standards and accountability in our nation's public schools, more than a third of black, Latino, and American Indian students in most public schools do not graduate.

State test scores across the United States have not budged the needle on NCLB's central goals, which target the achievement gap that separates white and nonwhite and disadvantaged children and their more affluent peers. In many places across the country the chasm on state test scores has widened as white students continue to outperform their peers.

Facing mounting sanctions under the federal law, many governors have made requests for a waiver that would allow hundreds of schools to avoid penalties for not meeting the law's ever higher targets. It is part of a national revolt against the law that forced schools to focus on measurable results, yet ultimately came to be viewed as punishing educators for not doing the impossible.

No Child Left Behind was intended to be the cure for the achievement gap. Educators were not being realistic. Large numbers of poor and immigrant students posed a daunting challenge. Mandatory restructuring, including replacing staff and principals because they had not met federal standards for three consecutive years, was required. Funds were taken from social studies and science classroom resources and fine arts classes in order to reduce class sizes and to pay for outside tutoring services and adding math and literacy coaches in an effort to boost test scores.

The strategies have yet to produce results on test scores and in many cases achievement gaps have doubled, especially for Latino and American Indian students. High dropout rates in urban districts assign many students to life on the margins. Under NCLB, progress has not come fast enough or far enough. The gaps persist. Changes must be made.

As this chapter on school culture draws to a close let us look beyond the reform to four concerns that affect school culture.

First, forget what you know about good study habits. Every September, millions of parents try a kind of psychological witchcraft, to transform their summer-glazed campers into fall students, their video-iPod bugs into bookworms. Advice is cheap and all too familiar: clear a workspace that is quiet, stick to a homework schedule, set goals, set boundaries, and do not bribe (unless in an emergency).

Maybe parents need to consider other issues. Does Junior's learning style match the teacher's approach or the school philosophy? Maybe the student is not a "good fit" for the school. Remember, teaching styles and student traits do intersect; so do personalities.

Let's take a step back. What is the big deal about learning styles? In a recent review of the relevant research, published in the *Journal of Psychological Science in the Public Interest* (2010), a team of psychologists found zero support for such ideas as visual learner, auditory learner, left brain, right brain, hands-on, etc. They went on to say that there is a lack of credible evidence that these concepts come into play.

Ditto for teaching styles, researchers say. Some excellent teachers caper in front of the whiteboard like summer theater Falstaffs; others are reserved to a point of shyness. Can we really identify any common threads between teachers about how they create a constructive learning environment?

Individual learning is another matter and psychologists have discovered that some of the most hallowed advice on study habits is flat out wrong. For instance, many study skills courses insist that students find a specific place to study, a quiet corner or room. The research finds the opposite.

Students who studied a list of vocabulary words, first in a quiet, windowless room, did far worse than when given a modern room with a view of the courtyard, music playing, and activity around. The brain makes subtle associations between what it is studying and the background sensations it has at the time, regardless of whether those perceptions are conscious. What appears to be happening is that, when outside context is varied, the information is enriched. This slows down forgetting.

Varying the type of material studied in a single setting, alternating, for example, among vocabulary, reading, and speaking a new language, seems to leave a deeper impression on the brain than does concentrating on just one skill at a time. Musicians have known this for years and their practice sessions often include a mix of scales, musical pieces, and rhythmic work. Vary your classroom study routine. What have you got to lose? You may find you have a lot to gain.

Second, school culture is deeply affected by negative stereotypes that affect learning, not just performance. *Science Daily*, July 27, 2010, published an article that said negative stereotypes not only jeopardize how members of stigmatized groups (women, African Americans, American Indians, etc.) might perform on tests and in other skill-based acts, but they can also inhibit actual learning, according to a study by Indiana University researchers.

One example has to do with women and their perceived lack of math and science skills. If this is not addressed, the reduced learning outcomes may ultimately hamper efforts for women to enter careers in science and math, where they are currently underrepresented. This study and others like it point to the importance of creating school cultures that reduce the impact of stereotype threat during skill acquisition.

Third, we must address a school culture that allows exposure of the letters *A* or *F* to affect test performance. Seeing the letter *A* before an exam can improve the result while exposure to the letter *F* may make a student more likely to fail. This study was published in the *British Journal of Educational Psychology* in March 2010. The researchers found that in most students' minds *A* means success, *F* means failure. Exposure to the letter *A* made the students approach the task with an aim to succeed, while seeing an *F* made the student concentrate on avoiding failure.

Students appear to be vulnerable to evaluative letters presented before a task. Adorning classrooms with symbols of achievement, such as *A+* and other success-oriented words and phrases may activate effort, pride, and the intention to perform well.

Fourth, our school culture needs to include social networking to save at-risk students. Maria Brennan has become pretty proficient at tracking down students who are on the verge of dropping out. So have Jose Sanchez, Kent Big Eagle, Mai Vang, and countless others. These educators have even snagged a few that have already crossed the line and helped them back into positive territory.

These educators have used a combination of traditional methods (reaching out directly to their students and their families by phone or home visits) and high-tech approaches (Facebook, Myspace, texting) to help improve graduation rates for their districts. The focus is on dropouts and truants and convincing them of the value of finishing school and earning a diploma.

When phone calls don't pan out, go to where the average teenager, and pre-teen, can be found these days: online. Educators are now setting up shop on Facebook, Myspace, and other social networking sites. Searches can be done through the sites' membership database by student name or nickname. If that doesn't work you can search on other students' "friends lists" to cross reference and find a more direct route to the individual in need of academic and graduation assistance.

Teachers firmly believe that showing students that you really care for them is the key element for preventing dropping out. Whatever means it takes to reach out to them is well worth the time. Having teachers who take the time to use this tool is an extra bonus for any school system. If each individual responsible for educating children (parents, school, and community) did their part, the graduation dropout rate would not be a problem.

Finally, no school culture can be developed without authentic leadership. Leadership depends on an ability to frame issues correctly, to answer the question "What is really going on?" and thrives when both divergent and convergent thinking are applied to issues. One must think divergently, challenging old thought forms by extending boundaries and making new connections, and convergently, synthesizing diversity into new structures and proposing new directions.

Leadership is a hot item today. Programs sprout up everywhere. Books, articles, seminars, and workshops abound. Like the latest diet fad, the current vogue for leadership produces isolated gimmicks or techniques, lucrative training programs, revised labels for old content, or worse, charismatic demagogues who tout quick societal or organizational fixes.

What can't be taught in leadership is good judgment. It is one thing to understand leadership, another to live it. Active leadership confronts diversity at every turn. The challenge is to reach across boundaries and to confront superficial unity in order to tap the richness of diversity. Leaders are agents of change and reform policies, persons whose actions affect other people more than other people's actions affect them. This is often ignored in our educational system.

A leader must be direct, coach, support, and delegate. They must have courage to be ethical. Know what you must do and do it!

Leaders in our schools must uphold the purpose of education, which is to invite students on a journey of mutual discovery. Exploring, bumping, challenging, and learning about others as we learn about ourselves. By confronting diversity you are challenged to explore your role as white, suburban, and senior citizen. You must also remember that fear extinguishes leadership and that courage ignites it. We exist between fear and hope.

Our mission for our nation is to demonstrate that people of different social and ethnic backgrounds, of all faiths and creeds, can not only live and work together, but also enrich and ennoble themselves and help build our future together. Our school culture must provide quality education for all, whatever it takes.

If you want to transform a school that has been stagnant for years, the last place you look for a principal is inside that institution. Stop thinking that students alone are responsible for low academics and start holding teachers, students, principals, parents, and the community accountable. Make the curriculum fit the needs of the student, not the other way around. Put egos and fears aside. A school culture should recognize effort, challenge people to excel, model, have fun, and keep hope alive.

Living and learning are inseparable. Students participate in the continued flow of experiences. As we reflect these experiences become knowledge. This process begins with the first breath of life and continues through the threshold of death.

School culture is merely a way of forming and organizing the learning experiences that society believes are necessary for children. School culture often is driven by expectations and requirements, whether imposed by legislators, parents, or textbook publishers. When that happens we need courageous advocates to step forward and focus on the needs of the child. Remember, change is disturbing when it is done *to* us, exhilarating when it is done *by* us.

Finally, we must not avoid the question as to whether there is a spiritual dimension to education and ultimately to school culture? If there is we must understand that spiritual questions do not have answers in the way math problems do. When educators ask deep questions, they do not want to be saved but simply to be heard. They do not want fixes or formulas but compassion and companionship on the demanding journey called life.

Maybe our questions are asked largely in our hearts because it is too risky to ask them in front of one another.

School culture needs to use anonymous heartfelt questions as a vital tool. These questions give educators immediate access to the wonder, worry, curiosity, fear, and excitement that burn inside our students.

School culture needs a deep connection to self, others, community, heritage, culture, nature and a higher power. Students who feel deeply connected don't need danger to feel fully alive. They don't need guns to feel powerful. They don't need to hurt others or themselves. Out of connection grow both compassion and passion for people, for students' goals and dreams, for life itself.

School culture should reflect students and teachers turning purpose into action.

POINTS TO REMEMBER

- The achievement gap between students of color and white students is over fifty years old.
- Culture consists of ever changing values, traditions, social and political relationships, and worldview.
- Testing is a school culture that may encourage cheating.
- Four concerns that affect school culture are study habits/learning styles, negative stereotypes, exposure to the letters *A* or *F*, and social networking.

Chapter Three

The Case Against Standardized Testing

Raising the Scores, Ruining the Schools

You can't teach a child how to think unless you have something for him to
think about. —Georgann Reaves

"Standardized testing has swelled and mutated, like a creature in one of those
old horror movies, to the point that it now threatens to swallow our schools
whole," says Alfie Kohn. In real life, plenty of people are being convinced
that standardized tests do not provide an objective measure of learning or a
useful inducement to improve teaching. What follows is a challenge to those
who defend the tests.

The more we learn about standardized testing, particularly in the high-
stakes incarnation, the more likely we are to be appalled. And the more we
are appalled, the more inclined we will be to do what is necessary to protect
our children from the monster in the schools.

Are we spending an awful lot of time giving kids these tests? Yes! While
previous generations of American students had to sit through tests, never
have the tests been given so frequently and never have they played such a
prominent role in schooling.

Exams used to be administered mostly to decide where to place kids or
what kind of help they needed. Now scores are published in the newspaper
and used as the primary criteria for judging children, teachers, and schools.
They have become the basis for flunking students or denying them a diploma, deciding where money should be spent, and so on. Tests are a mechanism by which public officials can impose their will on schools, and they are
doing so with a vengeance.

From an international perspective few countries give formal examinations to students before the age of sixteen. In the United States we subject children as young as six to standardized exams, despite the fact that many experts in early childhood education condemn the practice.

In short, our children are tested to an extent that is unprecedented in our history and unparalleled anywhere else in the world. So why do we test so much? For some a demand to test seems to reflect a deliberate strategy for promoting traditional back-to-basic instruction. Others are determined to cast public schools in the worst possible light as a way of promoting privatization of education. It would be logical to administer a test that many students would fail in order to create the impression that public schools were worthless.

Not everyone has ulterior motives for testing. Some just insist schools have to be held accountable. The famous *Nation at Risk* report, released in 1983, was part of a concerted campaign to stir up widespread concerns about our schools. Critics of the report say it was exaggerated and contained often misleading evidence.

Have you considered the influence of corporations that manufacture and score the exams, reaping enormous profits? These same companies then turn around and sell teaching materials designed to raise scores on their own tests.

It is fast, easy, and relatively inexpensive to administer a multiple-choice exam that arrives and then is returned to the company to be graded by machine at lightning speed. There is little incentive to replace these tests with a more meaningful form of assessment that requires human beings to evaluate the quality of students' accomplishments.

Testing allows politicians to show they're concerned about school achievement and serious about getting tough with teachers and students. Test scores are a quick and easy way to chart progress. The fact this way is by no means accurate is not considered.

If the public seems interested in test results, it may be due to our cultural penchant for attaching numbers to things. Any aspect of learning (or life) that appears in numerical form seems reassuringly scientific. If the numbers are getting larger over time, we must be making progress. We can submit that measurable outcomes may be the least significant results of learning.

Has the quest for objectivity led us to measure students on the basis of criteria that are a lot less important?

The significance of scores becomes even more dubious once we focus on the experience of students. For example, test anxiety has grown into a subfield of educational psychology. Tests producing this reaction are not giving us a true picture of what students know or can do. The more anxiety is likely to rise, the less valid the scores become.

Then there are the students who take tests but do not take them seriously. We have all had students who fill in those ovals in such a way that they make pictures. Even those test takers who are not so creative guess wildly or fill the ovals randomly and tend to blow off the whole exercise as a waste of time.

So on one hand we have a proportion of students who couldn't care less about the tests, and on the other hand those who care so much that they choke. Either way the test scores are not very meaningful. Anyone who can relate to these descriptions of what goes through the minds of real students on test day ought to think twice before celebrating a high score, complaining about a low one, or using standardized tests to judge schools.

We can even go so far as to say that the college admission tests (SAT, ACT) are not very effective as predictors of future academic performance, even in the freshman year of college, much less as predictors of professional success. They are not good indicators of thinking or aptitude. Piaget pointed out years ago that anyone could confirm how little the grading that results from examinations corresponds to the final useful work of people in life. No such exams are used in Canada and several hundred U.S. colleges and universities no longer require them.

Do these standardized tests tell us anything? The main thing is how big the students' houses are! Research has repeatedly found that the amount of poverty in the communities where schools are located, along with other variables having nothing to do with what happens in classrooms, accounts for the great majority of the differences in test scores from one area to the next. Only someone ignorant would present a ranking of schools' test results as though it told us about the quality of teaching that went on in those schools, when it really tells us about socioeconomic status and available resources.

Educators speak about worst tests. Critics feel the most damaging exams are multiple-choice. Students do not generate a response. All they can do is recognize one by picking it out of four or five answers provided by someone else. Complex cognitive problem-solving skills are not measured in multiple-choice tests.

Even essay questions leave a lot to be desired. They may require students to analyze a dull chunk of text, cough up obscure facts, or produce cogent opinions on a bland topic. What's more, these questions are often scored on the basis of imitating a contrived model (such as a cookie-cutter five para-graph essay) rather than tapping real communication or thinking skills. Pre-paring kids to turn out high-scoring essays can actually inhibit the quality of their writing.

The way these exams are scored raises even more concerns. These essays are shipped off to a company in Iowa or North Carolina where low-paid temporary workers (often noneducators) evaluate them.

Beware of tests that are timed. The premium is placed on speed as opposed to thoughtfulness. Be worried if tests are given frequently. It is not necessary to collect information or improve instruction through the testing process.

Protest if tests are given to young children. Students below fourth grade should not be subjected to standardized testing because skills are still developing rapidly and differently. Expecting all second graders to have acquired the same skills and knowledge creates unrealistic expectations and leads to one-size-fits-all teaching.

Be careful of tests that measure how kids stack up against one another (norm referenced). These tests contribute to the already pathological competitiveness of our culture, where we come to regard others as obstacles to our own success. Don't assign children to percentiles that help to ensure that schooling is more about triumphing over everyone else. Schooling is about learning.

To recap what has been said: the least useful and most damaging testing program would be one that uses norm-referenced exams in which students must answer multiple choice questions in a fixed time period and must do it repeatedly, beginning when they are in the primary grades.

Before we look at the real-world effects of high stakes testing it is worth considering that the approach is simply unfair. It holds people accountable for factors over which they have little or no control. Low scores are, to a large extent, due to social and economic factors as we've already seen.

Those factors include the resources available to the schools as well as the level of affluence of the community in which the school is located. It is unrealistic to hold a teacher accountable for his or her students' test scores when those scores reflect all that has happened to the kids before they even arrived at the classroom door.

In real life high stakes testing often drives good teachers and principals out of the profession. Teachers are tired of the pressure, the skewed priorities, and disrespectful treatment as they are forced to implement a curriculum largely determined by test manufacturers or state legislatures. Even if they stay, they become defensive and competitive. They feel the need to prove that failing test scores are not their fault.

High stakes testing has also led to widespread cheating. Educators in state after state, pressured to raise test scores, have been caught coaching students inappropriately during tests or altering answer sheets afterward.

This type of testing also may turn teacher against students. When a low performing child walks into a classroom, instead of being seen as a challenge, or an opportunity for improvement, teachers are seeing him or her as a liability. There is no longer a nurturing relationship that will enable trust. We have all heard of teachers and administrators who ask certain students to stay home on test days.

High stakes testing has radically altered the kind of instruction that is offered in American schools to the point that "teaching to the test" has become a prominent part of the nation's educational landscape. The content and the format of instruction are affected. The test becomes the curriculum. Teaching to the test is completely different from providing good instruction and assessing it accurately.

What does this mean for poor kids and for kids of color? We need to look behind the slogans and understand the reality of what high stakes testing and the whole "tougher standards" doctrine actually means for minority students, particularly those from low income families.

Senator Paul Wellstone (deceased) of Minnesota put it very well in a speech he delivered to educators in the spring of 2000: "Making students accountable for test scores works well on a bumper sticker and it allows many politicians to look good by saying that they will not tolerate failure. But it represents a hollow promise. Far from improving education, high stakes testing makes a major retreat from fairness, from accuracy, from quality, and from equity."

The tests may be biased, test design is questionable, and the quality of instruction declines for those who have the least. What makes more sense: to bubble in more ovals correctly on a bad test, or pursue engaging projects that promote sophisticated thinking?

Senator Wellstone went on to say: "We cannot close the achievement gap until we close the gap in investment between rich and poor schools. Otherwise we hold children responsible for our own inaction and unwillingness to live up to our own promises and our own obligations. We confront their failure with our own. This is a harsh agenda indeed for America's children."

If not standardized tests, then what?

Obviously we need some way to ensure that poor kids, in fact, all kids, are getting a decent education. So, how can parents be confident that their child is learning? To begin with, they can be given written descriptions (narratives) from the teachers, or better yet, they can participate in conversations *with* the teacher.

Parents should not be worried about a teacher who rarely gives tests; they should be worried about one who needs to give a lot of tests because he or she may lack a feel for how kids' minds work.

Parents can also learn a great deal about their children's accomplishments, what they're capable of doing and where they may be falling short. When teachers use performance measurement assessments, they give the students opportunities to demonstrate their proficiency by actually *doing* something like designing, conducting, and explaining the results of an experiment, speaking in a foreign language, writing a play, and so on. Ted Sizer and the Coalition of Essential Schools have provided guidelines for exhibitions, projects that reflect evidence of sustained thought and proficiency across disciplines.

One intriguing version of a performance assessment that a lot of schools are using is the portfolio. Students collect what they've done over a period of time, not just because it's helpful to have the material in one place but because the process of choosing what to include, and deciding how to evaluate it, becomes an opportunity for them to reflect on their past learning as well as to set new goals.

The bottom line is that parents should be able to see for themselves what their child has done. The teacher plays an integral role in this process, not only in providing structure and guidance to the student, but also in helping the parent make sense of how successful the student has been.

How does the parent know that the teacher's assessment is credible? Just remember that standardized tests aren't the only way or even the best way, to provide it. What makes more sense is a system that begins with the teacher's appraisal, basing assessment on an analysis of multiple examples of students' learning by the person closest to it, but then uses outside evaluators to validate the teacher's judgment and enhance parents' confidence in it.

As a parent, the best way to judge a school is by visiting it and looking for evidence of learning and interest in learning. Parents can also observe what happens at home. Are their kids excited about school? Do they read on their own? Are they using critical thinking skills?

We have to remember that learning takes place in classrooms, not in districts and states. To get a sense of how our schools are doing we have to start where the learning is and move out from there.

Each school should be encouraged to develop its own criteria for self-evaluation, inviting students, teachers, parents, and community members to decide what will help them determine how effectively they've been meeting their goals and what improvements can be made. How can we provide useful feedback to educators and students? What are the earmarks of a truly inspiring school? On what basis should we determine that a student is ready to graduate? Educators may disagree, but it is a start.

Ask yourself: Does everything depend on the quality of the assessment? More and more educators believe it's objectionable to use assessments to *make* teachers change what they are doing in order to be rewarded or avoid being punished. This is another example of doing things *to* people rather than working *with* people to bring about improvements. No matter how laudable the new standards for testing, they can't be shoved down teachers' throats. Teachers have to want to change.

Attitudes aside, educators need to be able to teach in a way that promotes creative and critical thinking. When disproportionate attention is focused on results, that is, on *how well* students are performing, this tends to distract them from attending to *what* they're learning. An overemphasis on assessment can actually undermine the pursuit of excellence.

Let's say you are persuaded that standardized tests are bad news. Is there really anything we can do about them?

It is discouraging to hear someone defend the standardized testing movement, but even more discouraging to hear someone agree that the tests are destructive and unnecessary but then adds with a shrug, "But like it or not, we're just going to have to learn to live with them."

Real children in real classrooms suffer from that kind of defeatism. The fact of the matter is that standardized tests are not like the weather, something to which we must resign ourselves. They haven't always existed and they don't exist in most parts of the world. What we are facing is not a force of nature, but a force of politics, and political decisions can be questioned, challenged, and ultimately reversed.

Equally disturbing is a blasé kind of fatalism that says in effect, "This too shall pass." Education has its fads and standards, but there is no guarantee that testing will fade away on its own. Too much is invested by now. There are too many powerful interest groups that are backing high stakes testing for us to assume it will simply fall of its own weight. In any case, too many children will be sacrificed in the meantime if we don't take action to expedite its demise.

Whenever something in our schools is amiss, when children are set against one another in competitions, bribed or threatened into mindless obedience, drilled mercilessly on forgettable facts and isolated skills, and so forth, it makes sense that we do something. We must do our best in the short term to protect students from the worst effects of a given policy, but we must also work to change or eliminate that policy.

Teachers have asked this question: If I am a teacher whose students are facing the prospect of tests that I don't really like, what do I do? The suggestion by many educators is to do what is necessary to prepare kids for the tests and then get back to the real learning.

The consideration to keep in mind with respect to test preparation is to do no more than necessary. Do not study only the test and distort your curriculum. Make it your obligation to make test preparation as creative and worthwhile as possible. Avoid traditional drilling whenever you can. Turn the test into a kind of puzzle that students can play an active role in solving. The idea is to help students become adept at the particular skill called test taking so they will be able to show what they already know. Always remember that no single measure should ever decide a student's academic fate.

What can we do?

Talk to friends and neighbors at every opportunity regarding test scores and focus on a child's learning. Attend school board meetings and speak out. Encourage parents to write letters to public officials expressing concern about testing. Challenge politicians, corporate executives, and others who talk about "raising the bar," imposing "tougher standards," and ensuring "accountability" to take the tests themselves. Investigate whether your state has an "opt-out" clause that allows parents to exempt their children from testing.

Despite all the educators who support rethinking standardized testing and even getting rid of it, our policy makers are forcing us to have to deal with more testing. Over the next few years, two groups of states, forty-four in all, will get $330 million to work with hundreds of university professors and testing experts to design a series of new assessments that officials say will look very different from those in use today.

The new tests, which Secretary of Education Arnie Duncan described in a speech in Alexandria, Virginia, on August 26, 2010, are to be ready for the 2014–2015 school year. He said they will be computer based and will measure higher order skills ignored by the multiple-choice tests. This will include having students read complex tests, synthesize information, and do a research project. "The use of smarter technology in assessment," Mr. Duncan said, "will make it possible to assess students by asking them to design products of experiments, to manipulate parameters, run tests, and record data."

Because the new tests will be computerized and will be administered several times throughout the school year, they are expected to provide faster feedback to teachers than the current tests. Proponents say that if these test plans work out, they'll turn the current testing system upside down.

The tests will rely heavily on technology in the classroom and for scoring and will be used as end-of-the-year tests and formative tests administered several times a year to help guide instruction. They will also include so-called performance-based tasks designed to mirror complex, real-world situations.

Experts say that teachers will be given useful information about what their students are learning and might require some mid-course adjustments. These tests will require teachers to adapt classroom instruction to make use of the tests and their results. This could be one of the greatest challenges our teaching force has ever faced. Here we go again!

Standards are important to many educators but we are beginning to see some of the sad consequences: teachers preparing students for the test rather than for their lives, teachers helping students cheat on the test, knowing that the standards can seldom be achieved honestly with the resources at hand, and states whose scores are a public embarrassment; therefore they lower the standards or abandon them altogether.

Hundreds of schools have taken their students and put them on trajectories much different than you would predict if you were focused on socioeconomic demographic backgrounds.

Look at which schools are most distorted by testing. The schools that best represent the current reform movement, like the KIPP Academies or the Harlem Success Schools, put tremendous emphasis on testing. They also have the resources to give their students music, dance, chess, Shakespeare, and philosophy. Most of the other schools in the country do not have any chance of success for their students when it comes to testing.

Testing should not be the end all. Let the schools become the lever in the process of change. The mission must transcend the test. Schools need to know what kind of graduate they want to produce. Schools that are most accountability-centric are also the most alive.

Desperate circumstances call for drastic action. Educators should not propose to make schools easier, but to make them better. We need to rethink standardized, high stakes testing.

POINTS TO REMEMBER

- Testing holds people accountable for factors over which they have little control.
- Beware of tests that are timed and measure how students stack up against one another.
- Teaching to the test has become a prominent part of the educational landscape.
- Schools should be encouraged to develop their own criteria for self-examination.
- No single measure should ever decide a student's academic fate.

Chapter Four

A Tornado Brews

Who Will Save Children of Color?

We don't have a child to waste. We will not be a strong country unless we invest in every one of our children. All children are essential to America's future. —Marion Wright Edelman

Who will save black children? Bob Herbert, columnist for the *New York Times*, said that when he was a kid his Uncle Robert used to say that blacks needed to "fight on all fronts, at home, and abroad." He goes on explain that while it was critically important to fight against racial injustice and oppression, it was just as important to support, nurture, and fight on behalf of one's family and community.

Reports for the past several years talk about tragic conditions confronting a large portion of America's black population, especially black males.

We know that the situation is grave. We know that more than a third of black children live in poverty, that more than 70 percent are born to unwed mothers, that by the time they reach their mid-thirties, a majority of black men without high school diplomas have spent time in prison. We all know this, but no one seems to know how to turn things around. No one has been able to stop this steady plunge of young black Americans into a socioeconomic abyss.

Next comes a report from the Council of the Great City Schools (2010) that ought to grab the attention of anyone who cares about black youngsters, starting with those parents who have shortchanged their children on a scale so monstrous that it is difficult to fully grasp.

The report, titled, "A Call for Change" begins by saying that "the nation's young black males are in a state of crisis" and describes their condition as "a national catastrophe." It tells us that black males remain behind their peers in academic achievement and that they drop out of school at nearly twice the rate of whites.

Black children, boys and girls, are three times more likely to live in single-parent households than white children and twice as likely to live in a home where no parent has full-time or year-round employment. In 2008, black males were imprisoned at a rate six and a half times higher than white males.

The terrible economic downturn has made it more difficult than ever to douse this raging fire that is consuming the life prospects of so many young blacks, and the growing sentiment in Washington, D.C., is to do even less to help any American in need. The only alternative is for blacks themselves to mobilize in a major way to save these young people.

Black colleagues tell me that the first and most important step would be a major effort to begin knitting the black family back together. There is no way to overstate the risks faced by children whose parents have effectively abandoned them. It is the family that protects the child against ignorance and physical harm that offers emotional security, and the foundation for a strong sense of self. It is this foundation that enables a child to believe that wonderful things are possible. All this is missing in the lives of far too many children.

There has been a terrible toll that racial and economic injustice has taken, decade after decade, on the lives of millions of black Americans. But is that a reason to abandon one's children or give in to the continued onslaught of those who would do you ill? One has to fight on all fronts.

My colleagues say that black men need to be in the home, providing for their children. The community at large, including the many who have done well, who have secured a place in the middle or upper classes, needs to provide support and assistance to those still struggling.

Dorothy Height, the longtime president of the National Council of Negro Women, who died in April 2010 at the age of ninety-eight, always insisted that blacks have survived because of the family. And she often counseled: "No one will do for you what you need to do for yourself."

There are some people already hard at work on these matters, but leadership is needed to expand those efforts. Cultural change comes hard, and takes a long time, but nothing short of a profound cultural change is needed.

Let the message go out that walking down the aisle, or just sitting on stage carries with it a great responsibility. But graduation can be great fun. Watching your kid graduate with honors can be a blast.

Black children can't wait for Washington to get its act together. They don't have the time to wait for the economy to improve. They need Mom and Dad and the larger community to act now, to do the right thing without delay.

This is not a fight only for blacks. All allies are welcome, but black educators stress that the cultural imperative lies overwhelmingly with the black community itself.

All children can learn! Yet the harsh reality is that systematically most states and too many districts don't provide the necessary targeted resources or opportunity for all students' educational success.

Unfortunately, too often we find ourselves focused on beacons of light with outstanding leaders that are doing a great job saving hundreds of children, like Urban Prep in Chicago, and Eagle Academy in New York, while not aggressively moving to systematically give other students the resources and support that make those schools successful. We cannot afford to become affixed on the spotlight and thus ignore the larger headlights from the train wreck facing our country by the millions of students we are losing each year. We have too often settled for the sweet taste of minor success over stomaching the bitter taste of the reality that without reform we are winning some battles but largely still losing the war.

Increasing the number of Americans with college credentials is a necessity for America to be globally competitive. Presently, only 47 percent of black males graduate from high school, far short of the trajectory and post-secondary credentials needed for our nation to be globally competitive. It indicates that systematic disparities evident by race, social class, or zip code are influenced more by the social policies and practices that we put in place to distribute educational opportunities and resources and less by the abilities of black males.

Currently the rate at which black males are being pushed out of the schools and into the pipeline to prison far exceeds the rate at which they are graduating and reaching high levels of academic achievement. A deliberate, intense focus is needed to disrupt and redirect the current educational trajectory for these students.

Research shows that from one generation to the next, equitable access to high performing public educational systems can break down the barriers to success and change the future trajectory of historically disadvantaged students.

Providing all students a fair and substantive opportunity to learn is critical for our goals of reform: transformative innovation, consistent progress, increased participation in our democratic society, and global leadership in a knowledge-based economy. We cannot achieve those goals while black males continue to be concentrated in schools and classrooms where there are few opportunities for them to excel.

The fate of black males largely depends on the opportunities provided in your state or community. By working together, we can build a movement that guarantees every child, regardless of race or gender, a fair and substantive opportunity to learn and fully participate in our democratic society.

The key to success, to averting these disasters, has always been education. The problem for our country though, is that we have been taking a narrow perspective on education. We need to broaden the way we see education so our efforts begin before kindergarten and extend beyond the classroom. We need to engage earlier and more comprehensively and then be willing to stay with them for the long haul.

To get there we need to radically transform the centerpiece of the students' educational lives, the public school system. Schools serving poor minority children are in the most urgent need of reinvention. Their failure is literally destroying innocent lives. Disenfranchised youth cannot afford even one bad teacher. Their families don't have the resources to compensate for that, yet they routinely get the short end of the stick year after year.

We must change our thinking to fit the mindset that there is no reason that the same black males who are heading for prison cannot be heading for college and to the workplace.

Yes, we need better schools, but we also need to address the problems outside the classroom that derail the education of too many black males. The achievement gap starts at birth, so we need to educate parents to take simple steps to engage and develop their children's brains in the first year of life.

We also need to strengthen communities so children have a safe, enriching environment in which they can learn and develop, where college and success is in the air just as it is in middle-class communities. It is the responsibility of the adults around our students to ensure that we level the playing field for the hundreds of thousands of children who are at risk of continuing the cycle of generational poverty.

Many black students are inappropriately removed from the general education classrooms due to misclassification by special education policies and practices. They are often punished more severely for the same infractions than their white peers. They are underrepresented in gifted and talented programs and few are in college-prep classes. The national percentage of black students enrolled at each stage of schooling declines from sixth grade through college degree programs.

New reports are emerging (Schott, 2010) that claim that black male students in good schools do well, and at the same time, that white, non-Hispanic students, in schools where most students are black have low graduation rates (Indianapolis) and also have poor academic outcomes.

As Linda Darling-Hammond has noted, schools and districts that have the highest percentages of disadvantaged students tend to have the least access to the resources needed for students to succeed. Thus, white students in schools and districts with large percentages of black males are also likely to experience poor outcomes if the district does not commit resources to such schools.

All too many districts and states in our country are allowed to maintain the intolerable situation in which they highlight and stand behind single academies or schools that are doing well while the masses of black students most in need of equal opportunities are the least likely to have them. The answer is to increase funding for schools in low-income communities and create a system of high quality preschool programs.

So what are some conditions for success? Equitable resources to support students to master rigorous content; universal, well-planned and high quality education for all three and four year olds; programs to address student and school needs attributable to high-poverty, including intensive early-literacy, small class size, after-school and summer programming, and social and health services; and state accountability to ensure progress in improving student achievement.

The American educational system continues to fail black males. To add insult to injury, black males are punished more severely, they are not in enrichment programs, and they are placed in special education. By grade eight relatively few are proficient in reading, and finally, as a consequence of these deficiencies, fewer than half graduate with their class.

America cannot globally compete or be a global leader unless we are able to identify by race, ethnicity, gender, and zip code, which person is more likely to have opportunities to learn. The platform for federal, state and local government, parents, faith partners, community organizers, and advocates must include comprehensive plans and policies that are necessary to provide the chance to learn.

Building one America, educationally strong, is our best shot at giving the United States and its youth an opportunity for success.

Everyone from Oprah Winfrey to Bill Gates has suddenly realized that a huge number of kids drop out and never graduate. Talk with dropouts and they will tell you that they leave school because they are bored, they feel invisible, or they have family needs they must attend to. The solution is not very effective. State after state has added more course requirements for graduation, leading to less flexibility for the engaging experiences that we know help keep kids in school.

The dropout and truancy issue is of major concern for our nation. The dropout rate in urban high schools may very well be the biggest but least known crisis in public education today. In many schools, 50 percent and sometimes more of the students who enter the ninth grade fail to graduate. As shocking as this may seem it remains a little known fact. Is this because most schools grossly underreport the number of students who drop out during their senior year?

The dropout problem has been characterized as a "phenomenon." Some educators argue that this is suggesting passivity. We tend to blame individuals for their own actions or inactions and not look at the structural factors involved. It is simply an institutionalized component in society. We need to first understand how it is produced and how it is sustained from one social context to the next.

There is a historical documentation of truancy, absenteeism, and tardiness dating back to 1872. By 1884, records showed that only one-third of the students who were required to attend public schools actually did. In fact, truancy and absenteeism was a widespread epidemic among students across the United States. Truancy has been a fact for more than 140 years, and large-scale intervention and prevention programs have not been successful.

Recently, truancy has been labeled one of the top ten major problems in this country, with absentee rates as high as 40 percent in some cities (Eric Digest, 2009). In certain Latino and African American communities in New York City, 80 percent of the students do not graduate from high school. On any given day some three million students may be absent from school and it is not uncommon for many secondary students to miss from twenty to ninety days in an academic year.

Truancy is not only a school issue, but a community one as well. Often truancy leads to a life of drugs or alcohol abuse, violence, and crime. Police departments across the country confirm that most students not in school during school hours are committing crimes, including vandalism, shoplifting, and graffiti. Truancy carries costs both for the children involved and for society more widely. They often leave school with no qualifications and are more likely to be unemployed and even to become homeless.

Truancy has historically plagued our society and is currently a concern for educators. Students who do not attend school fall behind in everything, which can lead to dropping out.

The fundamental question is whether or not educators have the political will to invest in the resources necessary to reduce dropout rates and eliminate disparities among racial and ethnic groups. The impact on the lower income populations is huge.

Advocacy programs are needed. Social networks are needed. Those areas that have some programs state that students transformed their negative perceptions about school and society into positive dispositions toward life.

The South Academic Leadership Student Association (SALSA) is a program in Los Angeles that targeted Latino dropouts. The SALSA program emphasized interventions that offered individualized attention for Latino at-risk students who were in the tenth grade, with the goal of reducing alienation, which many times perpetuates youth dropping out from school.

The interventions of the program included class changes, help with résumés and job applications, empathetic listening, counseling, goal setting, recognition for academic achievement, social and study skills building, tutoring, and referrals for additional assistance.

A second group that has helped with this issue is the Boys and Girls Club of America. This community-based organization is working to empower at-risk youth. Their goal is to improve problem solving and social/leadership skills. The founders had the vision of empowering youth by placing the responsibility of handling teen problems directly on the youth themselves.

The program is based on the principle that youth should have a space to talk with other youth in their own language in order to support each other and manage the difficulties of school, home, and society. The developers were convinced that adolescents who were neighbors, friends, and schoolmates needed the opportunity to work together to identify the issues that were crucial to them and to develop and express their ideas about those issues.

When students are given a forum to air their concerns about harmful choices they have seen friends and neighbors make, teenagers will work diligently and cooperatively to counter the self-destructive tendencies of their peers.

What is really wrong with our schools? How do our proposed solutions address the problems? Are any current efforts working? If not, why not and what more might be required?

The problem is not the "failure" of our public schools. They haven't really changed, for better or worse. The world has. No one is to blame, but we all share some responsibility for finding the solution. Our system of public education is more than one hundred years old. It was "invented" in response to profound changes in our society. The question becomes: How has our world changed?

The answer is everything has changed, everything except schools, that is. A rural, agrarian economy changed to one that was rapidly becoming both urban and industrial. At the same time America was opening its doors to large numbers of immigrants from around the world. We went from an unregulated system of one-room schoolhouses, to an assembly-line form of education that would standardize the delivery of basic skills, the three R's, to large numbers of students. We continue to give a large number of students a very basic education at the sixth grade level.

How has our world changed in the last twenty-five years? Well, every-thing has changed except schools. Did you know that the unit of study used in almost all American high schools today (called the Carnegie Unit) was introduced in 1906? It determines how the overwhelming majority of teach-ers and students spend their days in school, and it is still the way we organize information that is sent to colleges. Is there any other thing invented at the turn of the last century that remains in daily use in this country by millions of people that changed so little?

When our system was invented most people earned their living with their hands, first on farms, then assembly lines. For most of the last century work in this country required little or no formal education, and work involved little beyond following the boss's orders and showing up for work on time. Even as late as 1960 only 20 percent of all jobs in this country required training beyond high school.

In a very short period of time we moved from an industrial, assembly-line economy to one dominated by technology, information, and service. The skills are radically different. Today one has to have both intellectual and social skills to survive.

At the heart of the new economy is the information age. We have an information glut and the information is constantly changing. The amount of stored information is doubling every five years and is as available as tap water. The Internet has changed our lives. We have competency versus cov-erage. Many believe competency, what you do with your knowledge, matters more than coverage, what is observed, analyzed, and reported. In an age of instant access and information overload, mastery of real skills becomes more important than memorization.

Students should have competencies that are tied to work, lifelong learn-ing, citizenship, and personal growth. In the workplace one needs to use teamwork to solve complex problems, use technology to find and present information, analyze data, and create a personal growth plan. Under lifelong learning one should demonstrate the scientific inquiry method, fill out a 1040 tax form, make a budget, and open a checking account. Registering to vote and understanding how our government works helps one become a good citizen.

Students need good schools where teachers know their students well, curriculum is challenging and engaging, student voices are encouraged, real-world learning opportunities are offered, parents are involved, there is an emotional support system, the environment is safe and respectful, and there is a culture of data driven accountability.

One size does not fit all. Share the elements listed above, but tailor your schools to the needs and the interests of the community of teachers and families you serve. Allow for school choice. Remember that large numbers of children are suffering from the effects of education that is mediocre or worse. This does not have to be so.

One of the problems noted in education is that we teach people new or improved skills without altering or even discussing the original culture of the school or district. We need commitment rather than compliance. Create collaboratively through dialogue and inquiry the skills students need to learn.

As educators we have three core tasks ahead of us: Understand the context of education (how the world has changed), and then develop a vision of what students need to know. We need to create a knowledge-generating culture where we do not look for easy answers but instead frame key challenges and questions for us to work on. Finally, change the conditions of teaching and learning. Pay as much attention to improving the conditions of teaching and learning and raise it to a professional level. Improve conditions and build in supports for teachers.

Proverbs 29:18 said it well. "Where there is no vision, the people perish."

Success in school doesn't necessarily result from ceaselessly drilling students to prepare them for achievement tests. Noncognitive factors, such as students' sense that they fit in and are capable of doing the work, profoundly affect what they learn. Whether or not they believe they have the brainpower and social skills to make it in the achievement-oriented world of school can shape how well they actually do.

Students of color are especially prone to the fear of failing. As early as kindergarten, nearly a quarter of African American boys (three times more than whites) are convinced that they lack the innate ability to succeed in school. This fearfulness undermines their performance. They do badly, their fears are confirmed, and the cycle repeats itself.

We need to alter a student's understanding of the possible. If a student does better academically we all should respond positively. We need to replace the old pattern of failure with a self-reinforcing cycle of success. Students become connected and empowered and learn that choice and change are possible.

POINTS TO REMEMBER

- The fate of black students depends on the opportunities provided in your state or community.
- The achievement gap starts at birth.
- Dropout and truancy issues are of major concern for our schools.

- SALSA and the Boys and Girls Clubs are programs empowering at-risk youth.
- The Information Age has changed the educational mindset.
- Educators have three core tasks: understanding the context of education, answering challenges and questions, and changing the conditions of teaching and learning.

Chapter Five

ELL — Portrait of a Population

How English-Language Learners Are Putting Schools to the Test

> I do not know what your destiny will be, but one thing I do know: the only ones among you who will be really happy are those who have sought and found how to survive. —Albert Schweitzer

Amid national political turnover and financial worries, states remain on the front line in the push for school improvement.

English-language learners are a diverse and growing student subgroup. We must ask ourselves what roles education plays as a person moves from childhood through the formal K–12 school system, and into the workforce. What are the family income, parental education, employment, high school graduation rates, and adult education attainment indicators? All of this ties into how states are tackling the challenge of educating the nation's over five million English-language learners.

Nationally, the achievement gap between English learners and all public school students is significant. Those who score proficient or higher on the state math and reading tests are less than 9 percent. States vary widely in whether their ELL (English-language learner) students are making progress toward English-language proficiency. Arizona, Florida, and New York now require that all prospective teachers show they are competent to teach such students.

The No Child Left Behind Act (NCLB) has no provisions calling for teachers of ELL to be certified. Educators who teach students in classes in which the main purpose is to make them functional in English do not even have to meet the "highly qualified" requirements under federal law. As a result, no uniformity exists in how states and districts have dealt with the issue of hiring skilled teachers for the growing numbers of English-learning students entering their classrooms. The efforts are at best spotty, varying not only from state to state but also from district to district.

Immigration transforms communities. Jim D. Rollins had been superintendent of the Springdale Public Schools in northwest Arkansas for over ten years when the mostly white community began its dramatic transformation into a booming gateway for immigrant families and their non-English speaking children.

In 1990, the district had 8000 students and virtually no English-language learners (ELLs). By 2009, its English-language learners alone stood at 7000, roughly 40 percent of the total enrollment of 17,400 students. A thriving economy in and around Springdale over the past fifteen years driven by job growth at Tyson Foods, the world's largest poultry producer, and Wal-Mart Stores, Inc., the world's largest retailer, have attracted thousands of immigrants from Mexico, as well as a significant number of families from the Marshall Islands in the South Pacific.

"We had to be learners ourselves and we had to start from scratch," says Rollins, who has been the school's superintendent since 1982. "We started out by trying to train 100 or so teachers a year who would volunteer to go through language-acquisition programs in the summer, but it wasn't enough. With the growth we were experiencing, we needed to be much more comprehensive."

Springdale is the story of hundreds of school districts around the nation that have seen explosive growth in immigrant populations over the past ten to fifteen years that has brought non-English-speaking children into their classrooms.

Surging employment through the 1990s in industries such as housing construction, agribusiness, and the services sector drew immigrants, both legal and illegal, and their families to states like Arkansas, Georgia, Nebraska, Nevada, and North Carolina that had little recent experience with new immigrants and their social and educational needs.

The sweeping shift in demographic patterns has strained the capacity of school districts, and even state departments of education, to develop and pay for instructional programs to teach children who are still learning English.

Now, however, as a result of declining economic opportunities and heightened law-enforcement efforts around illegal immigration, demographers are seeing a slowdown in immigration rates. While the flow may be slowing, the population of immigrant families is now dispersed widely throughout the country and continues to pose challenges for states still learning how best to provide for their needs, including English-language instruction.

The U.S. Census Bureau reported that the number of foreign-born people living in the country in 1995 was 24.5 million. By 2005, that population stood at 35.7 million. In that same decade, ELL student population nationwide grew by about 57 percent to 5.1 million students, from 3.2 million. (Data from the National Clearinghouse for English Language Acquisition, based in Washington, D.C., confirms this.)

As the number of ELL students was rapidly increasing, the overall K–12 population remained essentially flat. This discrepancy between the two is what has brought this issue to the forefront.

The ELL population in North Carolina grew by 350 percent in ten years. In the 310,000 student Clark County, Nevada, school district, which includes Las Vegas, a surge in the ELL population started in 2000, when the district was already home to 19,000 English-language learners but southern Nevada's thriving casino and hotel industry and a housing boom sparked a new wave of growth that has raised the ELL student population by 8 percent a year every year since then.

Funding has been a major challenge in Nevada and other states. With the immigration issue being so hot nationally, funding for ELL programs has waned. States vary widely in how much of their own money, if any, they can or will allot to ELL programs. To top it off, all states are under pressure from NCLB to rapidly improve academic achievement for the 5.1 million ELL students we have today.

Some states dedicate no additional money to the task. Others set aside line items in their budgets. Given that enrollment is one of the main drivers of school costs, it's clear that the rapid rise in the number of ELL students, is contributing to the funding challenge.

The funding picture gets muddier. Instead of money going directly to ELL programs, many states allocate more money for certain categories of students, such as those whose families are poor enough to qualify for free or reduced-cost school meals, and some may count ELL students as part of that population. In addition, most estimates of school funding simply represent how much money is allocated to school districts, and not necessarily where, how, or on whom it is spent.

English learners pose a policy puzzle. The task of insuring that millions of children learn English, and succeed academically, is putting pressure on states and school districts as they push to boost student achievement overall.

In the nation's largest school system, New York City, the face of the typical student is that of a child whose parents were born somewhere other than the United States, and in many cases, someone who enters school speaking little or no English. More than half of New York City's nearly one million public school students have at least one foreign-born parent. The trend is spreading across the country.

Whether measured by state tests required under NCLB or by the National Assessment of Educational Progress, also known as "the nation's report card," ELL students lag far behind their fluent English-speaking peers in both math and reading proficiency. This is true even in California where there is a long history of educating children of immigrants.

The increase in enrollment and a shift in immigration patterns that have led many immigrant families to settle in suburban and rural communities strain the resources of the schools.

English-language learners are a distinctive population. School-age ELL students tend to be younger than the non-ELL population. The families are more socioeconomically disadvantaged than those of their peers. ELL parents do not have college degrees in many cases. Many live in low-income households.

Within the ELL subgroup, there is a great deal of diversity. A sixteen-year-old missed huge amounts of school days in her home country of Ghana due to an asthma condition. In the United States she does not miss school but is way behind. Another girl, seventeen, missed school while moving back and forth between the Dominican Republic and the United States, and lost a year of school once here due to pregnancy. Some students arrive in our country at age fifteen, sixteen, or seventeen and attend school for the first time in their lives.

ELL students hail from more than 200 countries that span every corner of the globe. Currently, Mexico is the largest single country of origin with Asia and Africa closely behind. However, about two-thirds of all ELL students are native-born according to the EPE Research Center. Also remember that some ELL students are at grade level and highly educated in their native language, others are not. We need to understand the subgroups within our population.

Kathleen Leos was Director of the office of English-Language Acquisition of the U.S. Department of Education before she resigned to join the private sector. She firmly believes that the key to a strong state ELL program is to align the academic content standards with the ELL curriculum. She also believes that all teachers who work with English-language learners must be equipped to teach language development and content at the same time.

In many school districts you find pockets of excellence and of mediocrity when it comes to ELL programs. The St. Paul, Minnesota, school district was commended in 2006 by the Council of Great Schools for nearly closing the achievement gap between ELL and non-ELL students. However, since 2006 the gap is widening again due to new state testing regulations. In New York City, data show strong academic gains for ELL students yet their graduation rate has worsened. The solution remains complicated.

Determining where an English-language learner should be placed at the time of enrollment and when the student should be moved is a key part of assuring student success. Under NCLB, states are required to develop a comprehensive English-language proficiency test that will measure annually what progress ELL students make in listening, speaking, reading, and writing English. Some districts require a certain composite score on the tests to determine when students are ready to leave the ELL program.

Choosing that cut-off point is a tricky matter. Most states choose a score at which researchers have determined that English is no longer an obstacle for students taking regular state math and reading tests. Presumably at that point, a lack of English is no longer a hindrance to doing well in mainstream classes either.

Georgia requires that all school districts use the same English proficiency screening test. Local educators decide what classes to give the students. In many districts there is no screening test and teachers gauge for themselves where students stand academically and where they need extra help. These teachers are attentive to educational gaps and help pinpoint strengths and weaknesses. There continues to be no uniformity across the country.

The challenges are huge. A seventeen-year-old from Guatemala could not read or write even in her native Spanish when she moved here and had repeated third grade years ago in Guatemala before she dropped out of school. She is now in our system.

Contrast this with Emilio, also age seventeen, who has much more formal schooling. He did not know any English but scored high in math and wrote well in Spanish. He is moving rapidly and making excellent progress in English.

Emily, a sixteen-year-old from South Korea had acquired some English in Korea and by the end of one year was English-language proficient. Thus, a student's English-language proficiency can have implications for the curriculum a student follows.

One disturbing factor connected to our ELL population is that students who are still working to master the English language are being held to the same reading and math proficiency targets as native English speakers. The challenge is to assess how well non-English speakers are learning the language, while holding them to the same proficiency targets as everyone else.

Many English-language learners who have been in school less than three years may have made great progress, but they aren't going to be at grade level. If you went to Africa and studied for two or three years and you had to take the SAT in an African language, you probably wouldn't do very well. It would not be because the school was failing or because "you wasn't" very smart!

A growing chorus of educators and researchers are pointing out what they see as a sometimes-glaring contradiction: requiring students still learning the basics of English to demonstrate their mastery of content on tests usually written in English. If a student is not at the level of proficiency to understand assessment questions, how would you expect these assessments to give valid outcomes for ELL students?

Under the U.S. Department of Education's interpretation of the law, recently arrived students whose English-proficiency tests grant them ELL status may be exempt from one administration of their state's annual reading/language arts assessment. Many educators see this one-year grace period as woefully inadequate.

Part of the problem is the test materials typically available. The assessments are mostly field-tested for mainstream students. Accommodations available are more for students with disabilities and do not help English-language learners.

There is tremendous diversity and the picture is made even more complex by variations within any given school or state ELL population. In the larger districts it is common to see between 115 and 130 native languages represented. Within each native language there can be a wide range of literacy skills. Many students have come from excellent educational backgrounds, but are tested in English, which becomes a measurement not of their mastery of the material, but of their ability to express it in English.

At the other end of the native-language-proficiency spectrum are those students collected under the umbrella term "students with interrupted formal education." These students have to learn school culture and test-taking culture at the same time.

The questions remain. What are we really trying to get the student to engage with—the English language of the test or the language of the content? What kind of supports are we able to provide ELL students without misrepresenting the content to the students or simplifying the content below grade level? What can we do to assess individual student needs?

English-language learners are putting schools to the test. If assessments designed mostly for native English speakers present an obstacle to ELL students, exit exams that determine whether students graduate from high school can be a brick wall.

As research has stated, it takes five to seven years for ELL students to be fully functional in an academic environment. This presents a major problem. Take the challenges faced by ninth or tenth graders who speak no English and have had little formal schooling in their home countries. It is not reasonable to ask them to have twelve years of education in the span of two or three years. To say that these students need to be proficient by the time they graduate is not a reasonable expectation. Many states still require ELL students to meet exactly the same graduation requirements as any student.

For some students, a fifth year or more of high school may be required. Under state law, students can be in the school system up to age twenty-one. But the NCLB law's cut-off for high school is four years. That can influence whether a school makes adequate yearly progress.

Students get frustrated. Not many eighteen-, nineteen-, twenty-, or twenty-one-year-olds want to be in high school. As a result, many drop out. All this depends on the literacy level these ELL students bring with them.

In recent years research has been focusing more and more on English-language learners. This new research is turning up promising insights on how best to teach English-language learners. Predictably the researchers found that the students who struggled the most with learning English lagged well behind their English-speaking peers at all levels of schooling, never really catching up at any point along the spectrum.

One curious pattern emerged among students with stronger English skills. During the first few years of school, this group's achievement levels were almost on a par with those of English-speaking students. But the more skilled ELL students began to drop back after fourth grade. By middle and high school, the gap separating them from higher achieving English-speaking students stretched into a chasm.

Researchers have learned a lot about how to teach basic reading skills in the early grades to ELL students. What they have yet to nail down is how to help this vulnerable and challenging population of students over the learning hump that comes later in elementary school, to teach higher-order reading skills, such as computer comprehension; how to teach adolescents who are new to English; and how to boost achievement in academic subjects other than English.

The bad news is that we're not where we're supposed to be. There is a lot we don't know. The good news is that the research is growing. However, the answers are urgently needed now. Our rank of non-English speakers is growing to historic levels.

To complicate this process, the existing research on the topic has been dominated by a single, politically explosive question: Should ELL students be taught, either initially or for an extended period of time, in their native languages?

Experts say that twenty-five years of independent research reviews conclude that teaching students in bilingual settings is more effective than teaching them only in English. There appears to be a lot of transfer that occurs from the first language to the second language. Even if the experts agreed that teachers should incorporate students' native languages into lessons for English learners, many districts can't or don't have the resources for such instruction.

Urban districts with large and growing populations of immigrants may have a hard time finding teachers conversant in Haitian Creole, Urdu, or the dozens of other languages their students speak. And seven states: Arizona, Arkansas, California, Connecticut, Massachusetts, New Hampshire, and Wisconsin, either ban or restrict the use of native language instruction with English learners.

It seems you can have bilingual instruction and do it poorly, and you can have English-only instruction and do it poorly. We need to figure out what it is you can do best, do it well, and worry less about the language of the instruction.

On the other hand, researchers widely agree that teaching the basic English reading skills to young English-language learners is not very different from teaching young English speakers how to read. When teachers instruct students how to decode words, how to spell, and how to recognize phonemes, which are the basic sounds that make up words, ELL students clearly catch up to English-speaking classmates in the early grades.

However, teaching students to comprehend what they read, particularly when it comes to more academic content, is another matter. We have done a good job of building up reading skills to the point where students decode words and read them, but they don't necessarily have the language abilities that would allow them to construct a representation of the text at a very high level. ELL students need to cultivate academic English as the language they need to succeed in subjects beyond English literacy.

English-language learners need to learn vocabulary words that are commonly found in print, but rarely used in conversational English or on the playground, words such as "predict," or "therefore," or "incremental." Take the term "photosynthesis." You can't give English-language learners the definition and expect them to get it if they don't understand the science behind the word.

Researchers are also zeroing in on oral-language skills in helping English learners overcome academic roadblocks. We need to encourage "talking the talk." Lots of ELL students are very shy. They don't want to use English in class because they're afraid they will be laughed at or they simply don't feel confident.

One way to prod students to talk more, especially in the academic arena, is to set up structured, cooperative learning groups so that students can practice speaking under less-threatening circumstances. ELL students should spend at least ninety minutes a week working one on one with carefully designed activities with students of different ability and English-proficiency levels.

The bottom line is that research suggests that ELL students need some sort of classroom support if they are ever going to succeed in American classrooms. Sink or swim does not work. Few, if any, modifications are being made to help ELL students overcome their language difficulties.

English language learners continue to grow in number, and we need to get serious about developing best practices that will build high-achieving students.

In conclusion, educators today focus on more than ELL. A growing number of educators and policy makers are asking about the effect illegal immigration has on our schools.

Illegal immigration—United States Code, Title 8, Section 1325 states:

> Any alien who enters or attempts to enter the United States at any time or place other than as designated by immigration officers, or eludes examination or inspection by immigration officers . . . shall for the first commission of any such offense, be fined under Title 18 or imprisoned not more than six months, or both, and for subsequent commission of any such offense, be fined under Title 18, or imprisoned not more than two years, or both.

We have a law.

Approximately two thousand people willfully ignore this statute every day, making illegal immigration a national crisis. Official estimates of our illegal population range from ten to twenty million, including school age children. Americans are begging Congress, mayors, governors, anyone who will listen, to simply enforce the law.

We are a nation of immigrants. But that doesn't mean to ignore the law. Activists say we have a duty to help the less fortunate. Others say it is not that cut and dried.

The truth is that over three billion people in the world live on less than $2.50 a day. The real question isn't whether we should be compassionate (absolutely we should) but to whom? Who's the most deserving of our help, those who break the law or those who have done everything by the book and still can't make ends meet?

It's easy to look at a family of struggling, illegal aliens and feel your heart break, but should they really have priority over the family of citizens who have paid taxes for decades and are now facing job loss, homelessness, or massive health care bills? If the current economic crisis is teaching us anything, it's that we can't help everyone.

America is a charitable country, which is why we've allowed so many people to sneak in here for so long with virtually no repercussions. But there is nothing charitable or compassionate about looking the other way while employers pay illegal wages and force workers to endure grueling hours in unsafe conditions. That is the opposite of compassion. It is economic slavery.

Black janitors in the hotel industry in Los Angeles once earned $12 per hour with benefits. When illegal labor flooded the market, wages dropped to $3.35 an hour, displacing almost all legal employees.

Common sense tells us that if you flood the market with lots of cheap labor, wages go down. It is a matter of supply and demand. If you *supply* businesses with millions of workers willing to take $3.00 an hour, then *demand* for higher priced minimum wage workers goes down. It is our Americans of color and the poor who are hit hardest by illegal labor entering the market.

Illegal immigrants are 50 percent more likely to use welfare than citizens, get free education, Medicaid, cash assistance for children (WIC), and food stamps.

There is more. Here are some harsh realities. Our nation spends more than $4.7 billion a year on health care for illegal aliens. California has been forced to close over seventy hospitals in the last ten years alone, due to lack of funding. About 17 percent of all those in federal prisons are illegal aliens, an astonishing number when you consider that they represent only 3 percent of the population.

Over the past twenty years the United States has invested more in prisons than in education. According to a recent study, *Cellblocks or Classrooms? The Funding of Education and Corrections and Its Impact* by the Justice Policy Institute, spending on corrections grew at six times the rate of state spending on education.

Remember, free room and board in prison is not really free. We are paying for them to be there as well.

We are also spending over $30 billion each year to educate illegals in our schools. This is money policy makers say we could probably use to figure out how to educate our own children since we appear to be doing less than an admirable job at the moment.

We really do have a dilemma in our country. We can't ignore our commitment to our English language learners and their needs. We also can't ignore the fact that illegal immigration is also putting America's educational system to the test.

POINTS TO REMEMBER

- English Language Learners are a diverse and growing student sub-group.
- The achievement gap between ELL students and all public school students is significant.
- The teaching of ELL students in bilingual settings is more effective than teaching only in English.

- Illegal immigration does affect our schools.

Chapter Six

Dangerous Schools

When Will We Stop the Violence?

As long as the oppressed remain unaware of the causes of their condition, they fatalistically "accept" their exploitation. —Unknown

Too many guns, too much crack, too few jobs, so little hope!

America has long had a love affair with violence and guns. It's our history, we teach it to all our youth stressing the Revolution, the "taming of the West," the Civil War, the two world wars, and on and on. Guns, justice, righteousness, freedom, liberty are all tied to violence. Even when we try to teach about nonviolence, we use Dr. Martin Luther King Jr. as an example, who was ironically killed by violence. Once we get past the rhetoric, what we really learn is that *might* does make right. Poor people have never had any might. But they want it!

It is because most people in this country don't have to think about their personal safety every day that our society is still complacent about the violence that is engulfing our cities and towns. Are we approaching one of the most dangerous periods in our history since the Civil War?

Rising unemployment, shifting economic priorities, hundreds of thousands of people growing up poor and with no chance of employment, never having held a legal job. We have a whole generation who serve no useful role in America now and see no hope of a future role for their lives. A new generation, the handgun generation, is on the scene. This generation is growing up under the conditions of war, war as a child, war as an adolescent, war as an adult, and war never ending.

This is not like Vietnam, the Gulf War, Iraq, or Afghanistan, where Americans, if they survived, came home. The war today is home. There is not even the hope of getting out. You just survive, day by day, hour by hour, year after year.

For the handgun generation there is no post-traumatic stress syndrome because there is no "post." What happens to people who never get out from under war conditions?

I've watched children grow up fighting with guns, and now they are young adults. The next generation could be called the Uzi Generation because of their penchant for automatic weapons. These children, armed better than the police, are growing up as violent. The gun manufacturers in their greed continue to pump more and more guns into our already saturated ghettos.

The violence is not new. Violence has always been around, usually concentrated amongst the poor. The difference is that we never had so many guns in our inner cities as we do today. This is the generation we are trying to educate.

Are schools in America dangerous places? Hundreds of thousands come to school with weapons. Schools often serve as gladiator societies for poor urban children. Intimidation, threats, and outright fights go on in classrooms, hallways, cafeterias, and schoolyards. Many students quickly learn that the teacher or principal might provide a sense of order when he or she is standing in front of you, but no one can really protect you in school except your fists, your gun, and your friends.

Even metal detectors, which may prevent a few guns from coming into the school, have no real impact on the students' sense of safety. The message simply states, "If you are going to shoot someone, it will not be in school. You just shoot them coming to school, or going home from school, but not in the building." Children learn early on that the adults who control the school are powerless to protect them.

How can a fourteen-year-old shoot another child his own age in the head, or how can boys do drive-by shootings and then go home to dinner? You don't get there in a day, a week, or a month. It takes years of preparation to be willing to commit murder, to be willing to kill or die for a corner, a color, or a leather jacket. Many of the children are conditioned only to kill and, more frighteningly, to die for what to an outsider might seem a trivial cause. The codes of conduct on the streets of our slums have always been hard, cold, and unforgiving.

With the influx of hundreds of thousands of handguns, you have a new brand of gunslinger among the young. Countless young people today are more dangerous than Jesse James or Billy the Kid ever was. Indeed, the Wild West was never as wild as many communities in Chicago, Los Angeles, New

York, Boston, (and on and on) are today. There is no Wyatt Earp, no one person or one program powerful enough, coming to town to clean up the mess.

It's handguns that make living in the inner city so lethal today. People have been armed and violent for a long time, but the weapon of choice used to be a bottle or a knife. The explosion of killing we see today is based on decades of ignoring the issue of violence. Every indication shows it is going to get worse.

Hit the ground, sound advice when someone is pointing a gun in your direction and you are not the primary target. Hit the ground, as all soldiers are taught to do when they come under fire. It is a sad state of affairs in this country when, starting in kindergarten, we need to not only teach our children their ABCs, but more importantly what to do when they hear shots or see people pointing guns. Hit the ground.

While it can be argued that America has always been a violent nation, Americans have been slaughtering one another at record numbers over the past twenty years, in what can only be called America's secret war against itself. This war's chief victims are our children.

In the late seventies and eighties the victims were thought to be almost exclusively poor and minority. More recently there has been a recognition that children killed by handguns are just as likely to be white and from working-class and middle-class communities.

Schools educate on the dangers of guns, metal detectors are installed and quick-fix conflict mediation continues. The ideas go on and on while the complexity of the issue of violence is ignored and the death toll continues to grow.

Most current policy makers fail to address the problem of the sheer availability of guns. Inner city youth know that a war is going on. Millions have been accidentally or intentionally caught up in the small battles that make up the war on America's streets.

As the number of guns available to young people has increased, so have the odds that they will be shot in a confrontation. Many have figured out that the best way not to get shot is to shoot first.

Has this country finally realized that violence is a national crisis? We sink billions of dollars into prison construction, more police, and talk about our "war on crime." Sometimes these large-scale initiatives have unexpected consequences that exacerbate problems instead of helping to solve them.

Look at the 1970s and the "war on drugs." When laws became tougher, the answer many dealers came up with was to use the children. The children were eager and willing to be used in such a manner. Poverty always provides willing children, whose lives are haunted by tattered clothes, empty refrigerators, broken dreams, nerves of steel, and toughened hearts.

Young boys associate the power and wealth of the drug dealer with the making of a man. These kids could operate in the schools as well as on the streets. If caught with drugs they would go into the juvenile court system, which was more lenient than was the adult system. Even if sent away for a short time, if he didn't snitch, he came home to respect and even more status than when he left.

As more and more children moved into drug sales, one of the first things they began to recognize was that they were in a dangerous business. They soon realized they needed guns and could buy them with their illegal profits. The gun was an added layer of protection.

Where once handguns had been relatively scarce commodities, in a very short time they became ordinary. The young dealers not only set a fashion trend with their expensive clothes and expensive gold jewelry, but they also began to set the violence trend. The handgun replaced the fist or knife as the weapon of choice. The codes of conduct on the streets across America were undergoing a major and lethal shift.

For decades it seemed that we in America saw nothing wrong with poor kids fighting for what they believed was right. Television and the movies showed outcasts as heroes. *The Dirty Dozen* and *Death Wish* and Bruce Lee were always willing to fight when the powerless needed justice. Those in America's ghettos worshiped at the altar of violence.

While violence has been a factor in our slums and ghettos for decades, never has it been so deadly. Today children face the task of making life-or-death decisions all alone, in a matter of minutes, sometimes seconds.

Let's face it young people are fascinated by guns. For many, the handgun is an integral part of their growing-up experience. It is as important to know the difference between a Tech 9 and an Uzi as it used to be to know the difference between a Chevrolet and a Ford. Once a young person gets his or her hand on a gun there is a very strong temptation to shoot it. They want to know what it feels like, what it sounds like, how much damage it does. For kids with guns, there is no limit on their power.

When dealing with the issue of young people and violence in our country, it's clear that we can't separate violence from all the other problems that plague our youth: education failure, teenage pregnancy, drug and alcohol abuse, lack of employment, crime, and AIDS; the list goes on and on.

We know we cannot design a few small demonstration projects and expect to have any real impact on any of these issues. We can't expect to make a difference unless we are willing to talk about comprehensive services for massive numbers of children *and* their families. We can't save children without making just as strong an effort to help the parents.

We must change the way we think about violence. Trying to catch and punish people after they have committed a violent act won't deter violence in the least. In life on the street, it's better to go to jail than be killed.

We must reduce the demand for drugs. "Just Say No" is a catchy slogan, but does not bring with it the kind of understanding of the destructive impact of drugs that a message from those whose lives have been all but destroyed by drugs can bring. At the same time that children are learning about the dangers of using drugs, they must also learn about the immorality of selling drugs to others.

We must also reduce the prevalence of domestic violence and child abuse and neglect. Too many children learn to act violently by watching and experiencing violence in their homes. Our society continues to turn a blind eye to domestic violence. The smacking, punching, or beating of women has become a routine in many homes. Teenage girls expect it from their boyfriends. In the same homes where women are being beaten, the children are being beaten also.

Our response as a society has been to wait until the violence has gotten so bad that the women have to go to a battered woman's shelter or we remove the abused child from the home. In both cases we end up breaking up a family. Would it not make more sense to intervene early and keep the family together?

Critics say that all we need to do is reduce the amount of violence on television and in the movies. Starting from the earliest ages we are bombarded with images of violence that seep deep into our subconscious minds.

It started with Mighty Mouse cartoons. In how many ways was the message delivered in that one cartoon series that when you have been unjustly wronged violence is an accepted response? There is no difference between the message that Mighty Mouse delivered and the one that Charles Bronson delivered in his *Death Wish* movies: when faced with relentless injustice you must act more violently than your opponent. In the movie *Dirty Harry*, Clint Eastwood killed without remorse as we in the audience, manipulated by the plot to believe he had just cause to kill, cheered his conscienceless violence.

Today, violence is even more graphic and the justification for acting violently is implanted more deeply into young people's minds. Cable television allows a child to watch violence day and night.

Many critics say we need to get rid of rap music. Sometimes rap songs are positive and many are simply kids telling their stories. There are, however, some rap singers who have decided that their niche in the music industry will be most violent and vile. They talk of killing, refer to women as bitches, and often bring a message of death and self-hatred. How about some limits on their access to fame and fortune?

Overall, rap music alone is not responsible for the explosion of violence we have around us today. Other media sources are equally guilty. The television, movie, and record industries should all reduce the amount of violence they sell to Americans.

Finally, to stem the violence we need to reduce and regulate the possession of handguns. In order to drive a car you need to take a written exam and then demonstrate how you are behind the wheel. You also need insurance. Yet you can buy handguns, which in some places in America are killing more people than cars, without passing any test of competency on how to use it safely, and without having insurance in case someone gets hurt. What is wrong with this country?

If we were fighting an outside enemy that was killing our children we would spare no expense in mounting the effort to subdue that enemy. What happens when the enemy is society? Have we failed our children? They live in a world where danger lurks all around them and many live in neighborhoods where their playgrounds are filled with broken glass, crack vials, and sudden death. Monsters are out there and claiming children in record numbers.

We must stand up and be visible heroes, fighting for our children. We must understand the crisis that our children face. We need to act!

What's the matter with kids today? Adults have been asking that question each new generation. We have always had kids that just don't fit in. Their school years are spent trying to fit in, be popular, be academically successful, and have a good time, simultaneously.

What has been going on in our schools? What has happened that made the nation suddenly sit up and notice that something seems to be wrong? How many incidents of student violence have occurred since the first media recording in 1927? The data are all over the place because some reports include suicides, others do not, some include only high school settings without adult involvement, and others include colleges and adults. No matter how the numbers are calculated, looking over the history of school violence is still a sobering experience.

The first recorded episode of violence involving a school was in Bath, Michigan, in May of 1927. A local farmer was angry about losing his farm, and to get revenge when he learned his tax dollars were going to be used to build a new school, he built a bomb, planted it in the school, and thirty-eight children, and two teachers were killed and fifty others injured.

The next recorded incident came in September of 1959 in Houston, Texas. A father was angry that his son had been enrolled in the local school so took a suitcase full of dynamite to the playground, set it off, killing his son, himself, two other children, a teacher, and a custodian. The principal and nineteen others were injured in the blast.

Until the mid-1970s it was rare that a student was the perpetrator in an incidence of school violence. As the years progressed, incidents continued to escalate. Some of the biggest headlines between 1974 and 2002 included: San Carlos, California, 1979, where a sixteen-year-old girl killed the principal and a janitor and wounded nine others; Greenwood, South Carolina,

1988, where a nineteen-year-old killed one student and wounded fourteen others; Pearl, Mississippi, 1997, two students and the shooter's mother were killed, seven others wounded; Jonesboro, Arkansas, 1998, an eleven-year-old killed four students and one teacher by firing a rifle from the nearby woods.

And possibly the most famous of all, Littleton, Colorado, Columbine High School, 1999, where two students killed fourteen classmates and one teacher, and wounded twenty-three others; and finally, Santu, California, 2001, where two students were killed and fifteen wounded by a fifteen-year-old shooting randomly in the bathroom.

Why is this happening? Easy access to weapons, prevalence of violent media, breakdown of the family structure, drugs and alcohol use, constant bullying or teasing, and growing involvement in gangs.

Who is doing it? The question is complicated. There is no solid or reliable profile of a school shooter. Just because the Columbine shooters wore long trench coats when they went on their killing spree does not mean that any student wearing a trench coat is suspect.

If a person is listening to violent rap music or playing a game of *Doom*, should he or she be put on a suspect list? It is a real balancing act to have a heightened awareness of what to look for based on previous evidence and still not overreact to students' behaviors, thereby stigmatizing, humiliating, or isolating them even further with erroneous labels.

What are solutions? A few that come to mind are: violence prevention programs, changing the school culture, avoiding stereotyping, taking a personal approach, using peer mediation groups, increasing security, using crisis teams, and having a zero-tolerance policy. The key to stopping violence in school is not a simple one. There is no single solution. Schools and communities must work together. "Let there be peace on earth and let it begin with me." Do what you can whenever you can.

Recently, research has found a possible link between psychiatric drugs and school shootings. Kelly O'Meara, a reporter for *Insight on the News* reports that many of the perpetrators of the high-profile massacres that occurred in American schools were taking the prescriptive drugs Ritalin, Prozac, or Luvox. According to O'Meara, these drugs have been known to cause psychotic episodes and violent behavior in some patients, and they may have played a part in causing the shooters to take violent action.

Despite the known negative effects that prescription psychiatric drugs can have on children, they continue to be prescribed at an alarmingly high rate. One of the Columbine shooters was on Luvox before he shot the students and then took his own life. Many of the shooters were labeled as suffering from a mental illness and were being treated with psychiatric drugs that have been known to cause serious adverse effects when given to children.

We can note that many say there can be a close relationship between prescribed psychotropic drugs and the subsequent use of illegal drugs, including cocaine and heroin. The United States has spent more than $70 billion on the war on drugs. Yet many concerned citizens are saying that if you think the Colombian drug cartel is the biggest drug dealer in the world, think again. It could be your neighborhood psychiatrist putting our kids on the highest level of addictive drugs.

Some pediatric neurologists such as Fred Baughman say there is no such illness as ADHD, no biological or genetic basis for it, thus no need for the prescribed drugs, which science can prove causes brain damage with long-term use. However, children as young as three years of age are being diagnosed with ADHD and these children, many of whom are not yet capable of putting together a complete sentence, are being treated with one or more psychotropic drugs including Ritalin, Prozac, Dexedrine, Aventyl, and Sytan.

Schools are forcing mind- and mood-altering drugs into the bodies on noncompliant students and punishing parents who resist. Does this seem crazy or not?

Maybe we also need to ask ourselves if our school policies are toxic to children's emotional and physical peace of mind. There is psychological maltreatment going on in our classrooms. Students are rejected, ignored, isolated, signaled out and picked on, made fun of through sarcasm and put-downs, and called names. They are ridiculed for their academic abilities and there is bigotry. Teachers simply say, "I was just kidding," or "Kids need to be put in their place," or "He's a big boy, he can take it."

There is ample evidence that psychological maltreatment in schools can be defined, measured, and prevented. Encourage children to talk to you about school. They will tell you about events they find disturbing or strange.

As we continue to look at school violence we also need to look at ethnic conflicts in the schools. In New York City, two African American students and later a Hispanic American student were attacked by white students. Their faces are stained with white paint. In Chicago, African American and Hispanic American students engaged in gang warfare injuring thirteen students and one teacher. Sixty teenagers were arrested.

The United States has always attracted people in search of a better life and a higher quality of education for their children. This trend, however, has led to ethnic conflicts not only in our society, but also in our schools.

Ethnic conflict is defined as conflict of any kind, from simple tension to physical fights, which arises between members of different ethnic groups, mainly *because* of their cultural and/or racial differences.

Our nation's public schools are among the places where members of the country's dozens of different ethnic and racial groups are brought together and required to work together more closely. The problem of tensions between different ethnic groups has plagued American schools for decades.

Why do these tensions show up in our schools? What can we do to bring peace to the classrooms? Will prejudice ever be a thing of the past? These are questions we should attempt to answer.

From its earliest beginnings, the United States has been a nation of immigrants from many lands. We are a nation which is made up of people who have left their homes in other countries to come and make a new home here. Even before we were a nation the American Colonies were populated by Dutch, German, Swedish, Irish, French, and English settlers. Let's not forget the American Indians who were here first.

In the 1840s, millions of Irish came to this country to escape a potato famine. Also in the 1800s, thousands of Chinese arrived on the West Coast hoping to help build the transcontinental railroad. Mexicans continued to settle in the territories of the Southwest (where they had been settling since 1600). Then in the first two decades of the twentieth century this country saw over ten million immigrants from southern and eastern Europe arrive at its doorstep, hoping to find a better life for themselves and their children.

One of the things that attracted many people to the United States was the prospect of a free education for their children. And so, the children of most new immigrants entered the nation's public schools.

In the early 1900s, a number of educators began to have new and idealistic notions of what the mission of the public school ought to be. These progressive teachers and principals saw the schools as agents that could help solve social, economic, and political problems, as well as educate children. They also saw it as their job to help new immigrants adjust to and become a part of the mainstream American culture.

The great wave of immigration that marked the first two decades of the twentieth century ended with an introduction of immigration quotas in 1924. The men, women, and children who came during those years adjusted quickly to mainstream American society. This was due to a booming economy, which made the good life possible.

Prejudice and tension around European immigrants subsided. However, in the years following World War II, an ethnic conflict of another sort began to build. This conflict, which would throw American schools into turmoil, would last for decades. This was the conflict between white and black Americans.

In the early 1950s, dozens of black communities challenged the notion of segregated education in our schools. This led to the Supreme Court decision, *Brown v. Board of Education*, in 1954. Legally segregated schools would, from that point on, be unconstitutional. A year later the Supreme Court ordered schools to desegregate, that is, allow blacks and whites to attend the same schools.

The remainder of the 1950s, 1960s, and early 1970s were times of conflict in the schools as various factions fought the court orders to desegregate. Civil rights activists worked endlessly to end the conflict.

By the end of the 1970s, the era of racial tension that accompanied the integration laws appeared to be coming to an end. In some cases this was because students and teachers had actually learned to live and work together. In other cases unsuccessful attempts at desegregation had left schools with largely unmixed populations. The 1980s and even the 1990s were years of an uneasy truce in the classrooms.

What's happening in our schools today? Prejudice remains prominent, as does name calling. Graffiti is another way to express hate, especially gang-related graffiti. Hate mail and more recently the popular Facebook web site promotes racial conflict. Violence, physical and emotional, is erupting. The increase of gang related activity also fuels the fire.

Before anything effective can be done in a school to solve ethnic/racial conflict, an essential first step must be taken. The school must admit a problem exists. Once that happens there are three avenues that can be taken.

Racial and ethnic tensions are highest when groups are isolated from each other. One way to reduce this tension is to increase the contact between the groups involved. Cooperative learning is a great practice. Students work together to complete projects and assignments.

Education is the second avenue schools can take to promote more harmony between groups. Black History month, American Indian month, Hispanic culture week, Asian cultural week, cultural fairs, and the like are great examples of educating each other about foods, dances, art, and heritage.

The third step is to offer prejudice reduction programs. These are programs aimed directly at reducing students' and teachers' prejudices. Included in this area is also peer mediation. One of the most successful approaches to reducing ethnic tension in schools is teaching students problem-solving skills.

"I think we can't go around measuring our goodness by what we don't do, by what we deny ourselves, what we resist, and who we exclude. I think we've got to measure goodness by what we embrace, what we create, and who we include" (Père Henri, in the movie *Chocolat*).

Another major crisis in our schools revolves around the issues of bullying, the bullied, and the bystander.

I shall remember forever and will never forget:

Monday: my money was taken
Tuesday: I was called names
Wednesday: My uniform was torn
Thursday: my body beaten and pouring with blood
Friday: It's ended

Saturday: Freedom

These were the final pages of thirteen-year-old Vijay Singh's diary. He was found hanging from the banister rail at home on Sunday.

Bullying is a life and death issue that we ignore at our children's peril. It can no longer be minimized and trivialized by adults, taken lightly, brushed off, or denied. Thousands of children go to school every day filled with fear and trepidation; others feign illness to avoid being taunted or attacked on the way to school or in the hallways and classrooms. Still others manage to make themselves sick at school to avoid harassment in the locker room. Children who are bullied spend a lot of time thinking up ways to avoid the trauma and have little energy left for learning.

It is not only the bullied child who suffers the consequences of bullying. Many children who bully continue those learned behaviors into adulthood and are at increased risk of bullying their own children, failing at interpersonal relationships, losing jobs, and ending up in jail.

Bystanders are also affected by bullying. These onlookers may observe the bullying, walk away, jump in as accomplices, or actively intervene and help the bullied child. All these options come at a price.

Breaking the cycle of violence involves more than merely identifying and stopping the bully. It requires that we examine why and how a child becomes a bully or a target of a bully (and sometimes both) as well as the role bystanders play in perpetuating the cycle.

A deadly combination is a bully who gets what he wants from his target; a bullied child who is afraid to tell; bystanders who either watch, participate in the bullying, or look away; and adults who discount bullying as teasing, not tormenting, as a necessary part of growing up, not an impediment along the way, and as "boys will be boys," not the predatory aggression that it is.

It is not only the bully who may terrorize and haunt our community. Some victims whose cries went unheard, whose pain was ignored, whose oppression went unabated and unrelieved, have struck back with a vengeance and a rage that have racked our communities with incomprehensible horror and sorrow. Others, like Vijay Singh, who reached what they felt was an utterly hopeless and irretrievable point, have turned the violence inward and killed themselves.

These were students who felt they had no other way out of the pain and torture heaped on them by their tormentors, no one to turn to, no way to tell; they made a tragic and final exit. We are devastated by this final act but the bottom line is that these tragic outcomes need not have happened. Bullying is a learned behavior. If it can be learned, it can be examined and it can be changed.

The bully, the bullied, and the bystander are three characters in a tragic play performed daily in our homes, schools, playgrounds, and streets. The play is real and the consequences can be deadly.

The scene is set: We have a culture that rewards bullies and blames targets. We have schools that pretend not to have a bullying problem, that have a well-established hierarchy of student cliques, and that have no effective policies, procedures, or programs to address bullying. We have parents who model and/or teach bullying at home, adults who don't see the suffering or hear the cries of kids who are bullied.

Bullies come in all different sizes and shapes: some are big, some are small; some bright and some not so bright; some are attractive and some not so attractive; some popular and some absolutely disliked by almost everybody. You can't really identify bullies by what they *look* like but you can pick them out by what they *act* like.

Bullying is a conscious, willful, and deliberate hostile activity intended to harm, induce fear through threat of further aggression, and create terror. It includes three elements: imbalance of power, intent to harm, and threat of further aggression. When bullying escalates unabated, a fourth element is added: terror. Once terror is created, the bully can act without fear of recrimination or retaliation. The bullied child is rendered so powerless that he is unlikely to fight back or even tell anyone about what is happening.

There are three kinds of bullying: verbal, physical, and relational. All three can pack a wallop alone but are often combined to create a more powerful attack. "Sticks and stone may break my bones but words can never hurt me" is a lie. Words are powerful tools and can break the spirit of a child who is on the receiving end.

Physical bullying is the most visible and easily identified. Relational bullying is the systematic diminishment of a bullied child's sense of self through ignoring, isolating, excluding, or shunning.

Bullying is not about anger it's about contempt, which is a powerful feeling of dislike toward someone considered to be worthless, inferior, or undeserving of respect. If we are to break the cycle of violence, we need to create circles of caring. We need to create an environment that is conductive to creative, constructive, and responsible activity. Rules are simply and clearly stated, consequences are natural and reasonable, and second chances abound. Smiles, hugs, humor, and praise should be offered to everyone.

Children learn to accept their own feelings and develop a sense of self-awareness. Love is unconditional. Adopt: I hear you; I am here for you; I believe you, you are not alone in this. Caring schools and involved communities create environments that show warmth, positive interest, and involvement from adults.

The bully, the bullied, and the bystander—we as educators can rewrite the script and create for our children alternative, healthier roles that require no pretense and no violence. We can re-channel the behaviors of the bully into positive leadership activities; acknowledge the nonaggressive behavior of the bullied child as strengths that can be developed and are honored; and transform the role of the bystander into that of a witness, someone willing to stand up, speak out, and act against injustice. This is a daunting task, but a necessary one.

As Margaret Mead once wrote, "Never doubt that a small group of thoughtful, committed citizens can change the world. Indeed it is the only thing that ever has."

Do old-fashioned school disciple and zero-tolerance policies really work within dangerous, violence-ridden schools? There are frequent visits to the principal's office, detentions, suspensions, and expulsions. These are the established tools of school discipline for kids who don't abide by the rules. These kids have a hard time getting along with other kids, do not respect authority, do not seem interested in learning, and are disrupting the learning of others. The strategies are not effective. We have a big problem here.

Are these students attention seeking, manipulative, bullying, coercive, and often unmotivated? Or do they simply lack the skills to behave appropriately? I believe that when teachers recognize factors underlying difficult behavior and teach coping skills, the results will be astonishing.

The wasted human potential is tragic. Students are poorly understood, teachers are stressed, parents are frustrated because of perceived lack of support, and administrators often have their hands tied.

School discipline is broken. Tightening the vice grip hasn't worked. Zero-tolerance policies intended to reduce violence appear to have achieved the opposite effect. Behavior issues and dropout rates have increased. Yet according to the U.S. Department of Education, Office of Civil Rights: America's elementary and secondary schools continue to dole out a whopping 150,000 expulsions and 3 million suspensions each year, along with countless tens of millions of detentions.

Behind these statistics are human beings, students, teachers, parents, doing the best they can with the tools available. Dramatic changes are needed to help them. We cannot keep doing things the same way we always have and continue losing kids on a scale that is truly astounding.

We need to understand the factors that set the stage for challenging behavior, then create mechanisms that are proactive not reactive. We need processes that allow for collaboration. We need to teach skills that help students regulate their emotions, consider the outcomes of their actions before they act, consider how others are affected, and use words to let people know what is bothering them.

Many of these kids have a developmental delay, a learning disability of sorts. In the same way some kids are delayed in reading or in math, challenging kids are having difficulty mastering the skills required for becoming proficient in handling life's social, emotional, and behavioral challenges.

How can we help? Access the factors that are interfering with skill acquisition and then provide specialized, individual instruction to teach students what skills they are lacking.

Just remember, a student will do well *if* he can!

POINTS TO REMEMBER

- Current policy makers fail to address the problems of the handgun generation.
- Schools are dangerous places and society continues to turn a blind eye to the issue.
- Research has found a link between psychiatric drugs and school shootings.
- Ethnic conflicts are increasing.
- A major crisis revolves around the issues of bullying, the bullied, and the bystander.

Chapter Seven

Children of Poverty

The Ongoing Debate

I hope that someday we will learn the terrible cost we all pay when we ignore or mismanage those people in society who most need our help. —The Hon. Judge Sandra Hamilton, Provisional Court of Alberta, Canada

For more than a century, the conventional wisdom on the question of American poverty has swung back and forth between two poles, depending on the tides of politics and the economy. One explanation blames powerful economic and racial forces beyond the control of any one individual. This belief held that it is the very structure of the American economy that denies poor people sufficient income, and so the appropriate and just solution is to counter those economic forces by providing the poor with what they lack: food, housing, and money.

The opposing explanation for American poverty is that it is caused by the bad decisions of poor people themselves and often perpetuated by the very programs designed to help relieve its effects. If this theory is correct, what the poor need is not handouts, but moral guidance and strict rules.

Each era of state-sponsored generosity toward the poor in American history has been followed by an era in which government aid was judged to be part of the problem, not part of the solution.

At the beginning of the nineteenth century, local public agencies offered poor families "outdoor relief," an ad hoc system that provided the poor with aid at home, whether it was food, clothing, or cash.

In the middle of the nineteenth century, outdoor relief came to be seen as encouraging idleness and dependency among poor families, and new restrictions were put on aid in order to promote the moral fiber of the poor. If the destitute wanted help, they were required to enter poorhouses, which were harsh, unpleasant institutions where they were expected to work in exchange for food and other assistance.

During the Great Depression, public opinion softened again. Poverty descended on so many families, including many that had been stable and middle class before the economic upheaval of the 1930s, that Americans came to accept that any family could become poor. It was bad luck, and not bad character, that created the need for government aid.

There was widespread public support for the robust safety net provided by the programs of the New Deal. Through the 1940s and 1950s, those public assistance programs remained mostly intact. A few individual states occasionally applied restrictions, such as kicking mothers off welfare when they were judged to be of questionable character. This usually happened when their children were born out of wedlock.

For the most part though, poverty retreated from the public's consciousness during the postwar boom, as the American middle class grew strong, affluent, and complacent.

With the election of John F. Kennedy in 1960, the dominant ideas on poverty began to shift again. Early in his presidency, Kennedy appointed a top-level committee, chaired by his brother, Attorney General Robert Kennedy, to investigate the newly discovered crisis of juvenile delinquency, a phrase used to cover everything from truancy and torn blue jeans to gang wars.

Delinquency, the committee soon concluded, was not an isolated crisis with a single solution. It was a result of poverty, and it could only be solved by a total attack on the problems of disadvantaged youth. Why are poor people poor? The answer was that the government was not helping them enough.

In the wake of John Kennedy's assassination, President Lyndon B. Johnson helped turn the ideas of the reformers into federal policy, declaring what he called the War on Poverty. He pledged billions of government dollars to aid the nation's poor. It was a hopeful moment but it didn't last long.

By the end of the decade most observers concluded that the war had been lost, done in by the war in Vietnam, which took huge funding. The riots that spread from one inner city to the next, enraging blacks, intimidating whites, and causing the political radicalization of many black Americans leaders, who by the time of Martin Luther King Jr.'s assassination in 1968 wanted not community job programs but full-scale revolution.

Also contributing to the disintegration of the reform effort were two government reports, issued in 1965 and 1966 that inflamed and later suppressed public debate over poverty by challenging some long-held liberal beliefs.

The first was a confidential internal memorandum by Daniel Patrick Moynihan. Its full title was, "The Negro Family: The Case for National Action," but after it was leaked to the media in the summer of 1965, it quickly became known as the "Moynihan Report," and just as quickly became famous for arguing that the deterioration of the fabric of Negro society is the deterioration of the Negro family.

In the report, Moynihan took great pains to emphasize that the high rates of illegitimacy, divorce, and single motherhood was the direct result of slavery and racism. He said it was the responsibility of the government to address the situation. However, several civil rights leaders condemned this report. They felt that it was simply the latest manifestation of the white desire to see African Americans as inferior, irresponsible, immoral, and sexually deviant.

The second report, "Equality of Educational Opportunity," was a public finding of the U.S. Office of Education, though the department tried to bury it by issuing it on a holiday, July 4, 1966. It too, became known colloquially for the name of its lead author, sociologist, James S. Coleman, as the "Coleman Report," and it too met with an unhappy response from some quarters, though nowhere near as intense as the one provoked by Moynihan's work.

The report, mandated by the 1964 Civil Rights Act, was explicitly intended to demonstrate that educational opportunities in the United States were racially unequal. Instead, it concluded the opposite; while just a decade earlier, predominantly black schools were indeed under-funded, black and white students now received approximately equal resources.

Just as surprising, Coleman and his coauthors determined that a school's financial resources were not the main contributing factor to a child's educational success. It was the child's family background that made the more significant difference.

Together, these reports pointed toward the importance of the home environment in the negative outcomes experienced by many poor children. They also demonstrated the political danger in reaching such controversial conclusions. The Coleman Report was greeted mostly with silence or dismissal, the Moynihan Report with angry denunciations.

Into the vacuum came a new generation of conservative scholars, led by Charles Murray, a social scientist who wrote *Losing Ground*, published in 1984. Murray offered a counterhistory of poverty in America and again asked the question: Why are poor people poor?

Murray's answer was that government was helping them too much. He argued that the Great Society programs that grew out of the War on Poverty, like Aid to Families with Dependent Children (AFDC) failed to help poor people, and they actually hurt poor people. He argued that the existing system of aid to the needy provided an array of perverse incentives that encouraged poor people not to work, not to marry, and to have children at an early age, out of wedlock.

His solution was drastic. He proposed scrapping the entire federal welfare system and income-support structures like AFDC, Medicaid, food stamps, unemployment insurance, workers compensation, subsidized housing, disability insurance, and everything else.

Murray's book finally awakened the liberal thinkers who had been reluctant to draw attention to the disaster that was brewing in the nation's ghettos. These policy makers said that government was not the cause. Instead African Americans in the inner city were the victims of a series of tectonic shifts in society and economy since the end of World War II.

Harlem was cited as an example. In 1900, it was an affluent white neighborhood. Then blacks moved in and whites moved out. By 1960 even the more affluent blacks were moving out to the suburbs, leaving a ghetto behind. This was happening across the nation.

At the same time, the American manufacturing economy was experiencing a rapid decline, and the kind of low-skill jobs that had sustained many urban African American families were disappearing. They were replaced with white-collar jobs and these jobs required a level of education that our system discouraged black families from achieving.

By 1984, for the first time, a gap opened up between African American and white employment figures, especially among young adults, and it quickly grew. A brand new kind of urban ghetto, almost all black and poor, opened up. Other social dysfunctions followed: large numbers of recipients of government aid, high crime rates, high teenage birth rates, and low marriage rates.

The exodus of middle-class and working-class families from neighborhoods like Harlem had removed a social buffer. In poor communities during economic downturns the presence of middle-class families once provided mainstream role models that helped keep alive the perception that education is meaningful, that steady employment is a noble alternative to welfare, and that family stability is the norm, not the exception.

But in a ghetto neighborhood where those families have left, there would be a ripple effect leading to social dislocation. Children would not be able to interact with people who were employed. Joblessness became a way of life. Teachers became frustrated and did not teach. The children did not learn.

These liberal policymakers suggested a child support assurance program, childcare assistance, and a family allowance program. They also believed that government needed to overhaul the national economy completely, not just tinker around the edges. Many wanted a social democracy in which the federal government would guarantee a wide range of financial supports to every American family.

These policy makers established the parameters for the next fifteen years in the public debate over poverty. There were Reagan-era cutbacks in government aid for the poor. Reforms of the welfare system were passed in the mid-1990s. They all agreed that the lives of those in the ghetto were deeply affected by decisions made in Washington, D.C.

If the right set of incentives and opportunities were dangled in front of poor ghetto residents, they would respond by getting jobs, become better educated, would be more likely to marry, and raise their children more conscientiously. Policy makers also acknowledged that the dysfunction of ghetto families was the result of decades and generations of discrimination, isolation, and cultural decay.

In 1994, Charles Murray published another book, *The Bell Curve*, in which he said the cause of the persistent achievement gap between rich and poor children and black and white children was not federal welfare policy at all. It was deep-rooted differences in intelligence.

The book's thesis was based on three observations: the economy had changed in a way that caused intelligence to be more highly valued, the IQ of rich people tends to be higher than that of poor people, and the IQ of children is closely related to the IQ of their parents. Educators agreed. They felt the book demonstrated in a coherent and thorough way how important the results on standardized tests had become. A child's success depended on something tangible, measurable, and teachable.

In the ongoing debate over poverty in America, this was great news. It was a new answer to the central question: Why are poor people poor? They are poor, this evidence suggested, not because of government aid, not because they are genetically flawed, and not because the system denies them opportunities, but because they lack certain specific skills.

In some ways this seemed obvious. Of course poor people lack many skills, and of course people with skills do better in life. But the close connection between abilities and outcomes was something new. Black families bought into this idea.

The extended economic recovery of the 1990s proved that a booming economy and a healthy job market would do much to alleviate poverty. Then why did statistics out of Harlem show how much things hadn't changed, especially for those at the bottom?

The generational cycle of poverty in neighborhoods like Harlem is well known: poor parents raise children with poor resources and abilities, who therefore can't make it out of poverty and thus raise their own children with the same problems.

In the early 2000s human capital (skills and abilities) became an increasingly popular way to look at the problem of poverty. New questions arose: What specific resources did middle-class children have that allowed them to succeed at such higher rates than poor children? What skills did poor children need to help them compete? What interventions in their lives and parents' lives could help them acquire those skills? Forget the way human policies make you feel. Instead examine what different policies and interventions actually accomplish.

Educators jumped on board and said to stop blaming the victims of poverty by claiming that their situation was due to some personal shortcoming. Their deficits, whether they were in income or knowledge, esoteric qualities like self-control or perseverance, or an optimistic outlook were not moral failings. Poor children are just like other children; they were just missing certain resources, knowledge, and skills.

The question becomes: which of these obstacles (bad schools, bad nutrition, fewer books, parents less educated) can the child cope with, and which do educators need to remove?

One fact stands out in academic research. The gap began when children were very young. By the time they started kindergarten, there was already a large difference between poor and rich children. Something was going wrong in the homes and families and neighborhoods of poor children before they set foot in a school building.

Do we even dare consider the idea that changing the way parents deal with their children may be the single most important thing we can do to improve children's cognitive skills. Researchers say that by the age of three children of professional parents have a vocabulary of about 1,100 words and children of parents on welfare have a vocabulary of 525 words. This correlates to the number of words the parent spoke to the child.

Researchers also discovered that by the age of three, the average professional child would hear about 500,000 encouragements and 80,000 discouragements. For the welfare child, the ratio was reversed: 80,000 encouragements and 200,000 discouragements (Murray, 2010).

Some researchers set out to see what effect attitudes, beliefs, and values passed down by families had on academic success. They found that in middle-class families, parents considered a child's development their responsibility, so they planned and scheduled countless activities to enhance that development, such as piano lessons, soccer games, and trips to museums and engaged their children as equals in conversations, encouraging questions. The working class and poor families did things very differently. They allowed their children much more freedom to fill their weekends and afternoons as they chose.

All kids might start out at birth the same way but from the first days of life, middle-class children tend to receive extra stimulation and support, allowing them to develop and hone those skills that they need to succeed in school.

Do schools need to enter the realm of looking at the practices and philosophies of American parenting as Geoffrey Canada did when creating his Harlem Children's Zone? His philosophy in creating a ninety-seven block laboratory in central Harlem where he is testing new and often controversial ideas about poverty in America is this: If you want poor kids to be able to compete with their middle-class peers, you need to change everything in their lives, their schools, their neighborhoods, and even the child-rearing practices of their parents.

Canada had already concluded that if he wanted to change the lives of Harlem's poor children, then starting at kindergarten was too late. He put together a bare-bones curriculum for a new parenting-skills program in Harlem, the Baby College.

He created classes for new teenage parents and parents-to-be. Young mothers saw the program as a second chance, a way to correct mistakes their mothers had made. Class participants were urged to talk about how they were raised and if they intended to parent in the same way. The major part of the mission of the Baby College was to figure out what advice and support to give these parents so that their children would have a better chance at success.

Culture is very strong when it comes to child-rearing practices. Many believe good kids are quiet kids. If you are a good parent your child listens to you; if you are a bad parent your kid doesn't. The problem is that no two-year-old listens to anyone.

The Baby College also stressed a different approach to discipline. Many parents were hit as children, and they learned to replace physical punishment with a system of rules enforced by talk, negotiation, rewards, withdrawal of privileges, and time-outs.

There must also be the realization that some parents have substance abuse and mental health issues. A conversation in a classroom will not solve that. Outside services may need to be called in to help.

If we are going to tackle this issue of parenting we must remember that whites cannot tell black parents or any parent of color to change their practices without provoking charges of ethnocentrism, racism, and much more. The idea is not to adopt middle-class white culture or even to imitate it. The idea is to think, borrow some tricks, and adapt.

The real goal of parenting programs is not to impart information. It is to change the parents' whole vision of themselves as parents, to encourage them to accept the idea that their child's education and intellectual development begins at birth, if not before. They as parents have a crucial role to play in that development.

The relationship between race and poverty in the United States has long been a complicated one. We find more poor white Americans than poor black Americans. However, black Americans are more likely to be consistently poor for a longer period; when whites experience poverty, it is more likely to be for a limited time.

Black poverty has different characteristics than white poverty. Downward mobility is more common. Often children of solidly middle-class black families slip into poverty as adults. Poor black Americans and other families of color live in high-poverty neighborhoods. Most live below the poverty line. They do not prepare their children to be educated.

Many families of color believe that education is something that takes place in school, when you're sitting down at a desk with a pen and notebook. However, we are finding pockets of very involved and focused parents who want to cram education into almost every moment. Life becomes a race. These parents are doing everything possible to give their children a jump-start in that race.

Dysfunctional families and poverty are no excuse for widespread, chronic, educational failure. The unfortunate circumstances of students in inner city neighborhoods simply make educating these children more of a challenge. The real problem appears to be a school system that does not educate poor children. Poor minority students can succeed if they are immersed in an educational environment that is demanding, disciplined, and well run.

When we examine educational policy we must be willing to take a stand for vouchers, for charter schools, for anything that blows up the status quo. Ask yourselves if the people who care about education the most, who really want to see it work, are the ones destroying it. Those of us who have been in the trenches every day may want to blow it up, too.

Schools may not be able to do everything on their own but could do a whole lot more than they are. Many students are the victims of years of educational neglect. They are often written off too early by a system that uses as an excuse the idea that it is impossible to educate poor children. Whatever you may think, it is never too late. Expose the students to a whole lot more instruction. Extend the school day if necessary, the year if you have to. The clock is ticking.

If a student is missing several days of school, treat it like a crisis. Absenteeism is a huge problem and everyone in the school should think of it as their problem. Change your attitude from: How much can we afford to do? to one of: How much do we need to do? Start from the result you want to achieve, however improbable, and then work backward, figuring out everything you have to do in order to get there.

The gravity of the community always pulls the child down. Lousy schools, lousy neighborhoods, the stress of being poor all begin to weigh on that child and that family. What would it take to get an entire community of poor children born to poorly educated, overburdened parents to college, to turn them all into functioning members of the American middle-class?

Our goal is to elevate these kids to the top rungs of academic achievement and steer them away from crime and violence. Impact the community by encouraging college, encouraging success.

If poverty is considered a disease that infests an entire community in the form of unemployment and violence, failing schools, and broken homes, then we can't treat those symptoms in isolation. We have to heal that entire community. We have to focus on what works.

Why don't we give every child the tools to succeed? Why not level the playing field for real? In the past, there had always been someone there with an answer, an explanation for why it couldn't be done, or why the question didn't make sense, or why the time just wasn't right. We need change. We need more people who will answer the question.

As a country we need to realize what a mistake it is not to nourish children of poverty. These children have courage, ingenuity, eagerness to learn, trust, compassion for others, and genuine kindness.

If we can locate the young people who need help the most, why do we not target our resources and focus our concern on improving the system by working on the students who are at the highest risk of school failure? The best way to deal with this problem is to provide a seamless web of services, combining education, health care, housing, transportation, and social welfare.

During early adolescence poor inner city youth become aware of the biting divide between how they live and how the rest of the American society lives. Also during this period, seeds of despair, crime, joblessness, incarceration, and death take root. Many conclude that the world is indifferent to their existence.

For most inner city youth the shift is greatly influenced by their schooling and whatever value they attach to it. Feelings of alienation and ambivalence toward formal education are cultivated. All of a sudden they realize that being somebody is directly attached to the peer culture around them than to the classroom. The intersections between socioeconomic resources, geographical location, ethnicity, and race are critical here as they demonstrate groups who are more at risk of school failure.

The conventional understanding is that school prepares young people for the future. So often they are told, "Stay in school and get your education." However, urban youth are apt to hear this message from individuals who have not taken advantage of their own education. For urban youth growing up in an environment where many adults have been defaulted by school intentionally or unintentionally, the value of school to one's future is seen as a false promise. They often resist the idea that schooling has value especially if instruction fails to be responsive to their needs.

We must remember that many poor students are too preoccupied with thoughts of their own mortality and the day-to-day energy required to survive to think about education as a bridge to the future. You can hear it in their music. You can hear it in their writing. You can hear the preoccupation with death in their conversations.

Education must have value in these young people's current time and space if it is to attract their time and attention. Education must address their issues and concerns in a way that will lead them to examine their own lives.

We all know that education can lead to college enrollment, lower levels of unemployment, a reduction in violent crime, and lower incarceration rates. However, urban youth are skeptical that education can help them escape from their poverty. Many believe that their fate has been determined and that failure is inevitable. The turmoil in their lives is so intense they are unable to see beyond it, and they do not believe anyone cares about them.

Curricula and educational plans have fallen short of addressing the academic, cultural, emotional, and social needs of our urban youth. Many are seeking a balance between taking their minds off the pain of poverty and sustaining hope for the future. Poverty has a way of souring their childhood. Education can sweeten it.

Caring teachers with high expectations can be a way out. They can help push against the currents of the environment. These teachers don't care if you live below the poverty level. They do not lower expectations and do not limit their aspirations for the students. Caring teachers have Harvard dreams for the student living in hellish conditions.

Fortunately, some Americans care. Three out of every four voters agree that our schools need help. Our political leaders are not doing enough to help solve the problems facing our children. Despite strong concern over our national debt, two-thirds of the American people are saying that government programs for children should be the last to be cut. This willingness to help children extends to voters of all ages, races, and political and economic backgrounds.

We can make a difference for a child. In helping children pull themselves out of poverty, society benefits too. Crime rates go down, children become better educated, and then see their futures with more optimistic eyes. One of the major benefits of working with children is seeing tangible results: from their smiling, "I can do it" faces to increased academic scores.

Please encourage your students to take this oath. "I promise to always dream out loud. I will lift my head and be proud. And never, never end up a face in the crowd."

It works!

POINTS TO REMEMBER

- Ask yourself: Why are poor people poor?
- By the time students start kindergarten there is already a huge difference between poor and rich children.
- The goal of parenting programs should be to change the parents' vision of themselves, not just to give information.
- Education must address the issues and needs of students of poverty.

Chapter Eight

Who Influences Education in America? Can Anyone?

Public education is the cornerstone of our democracy. It must be our first priority in every community, for every child. —PEN (Public Education Network)

John Merrow, reporter and producer of education pieces for the *PBS News Hour* and other documentaries recently speculated (as he put it) about the most influential person in American education. This was the result of his post on July 6, 2011: At the top of his original list of influential people: Wendy Kopp, the founder of Teach for America; education secretary, Arnie Duncan; former New York schools chancellor, Joel Klein, for his remarkable network of eleven protégés now influencing what happens in schools and classrooms around the nation; Diane Ravitch, for her ongoing leadership in the education wars; and Big Bird.

Forget the quibble that one of the original five was not a person, and that three have never worked in a K–12 classroom. What about Bill and Melinda Gates or Eli Broad and the foundations they created with billions of dollars? What about former Washington, D.C., superintendent, Michelle Rhee, who was determined to beat up on teacher unions?

How many of us can name, much less agree on, the most influential people in education in 2001 or in 1991? George W. Bush, Rod Paige, Bill Bennett, Richard Riley, Linda Darling-Hammond, Arthur Levin? Or for that matter, name anyone in all of American history, other than maybe Thomas Jefferson, Horace Mann, or John Dewey, who was a great national influence on education? Parson Weems, Milton Friedman, Ellwood Cubberly, Mark Hopkins?

Are there people around like James Conant today? James Conant (1893–1978) was an educator and scientist and was challenged by national issues in education. He explored the role of education in a democracy after World War I because he wanted to identify leaders who could forward the aims of the democratic tradition. He sought to combine the education and training of the general population with a system that saw as its first priority the identification and development of the talented few. He believed an educational elite leading informed and trained masses would best serve the country's democracy.

After twenty years at the helm of Harvard, he left for the private sector, to serve in Germany as high commissioner and ambassador, managing the occupying military forces. In 1957 he returned to the field of education using his prestige and national visibility to strengthen schooling at its core, public education.

Conant advocated for a separate and more rigorous academic path for talented youth. In 1961 he wrote *Slums and Suburbs* and referred to the developing "social dynamite" accumulating in the nation's large cities and advocated improvement of schools in geographic area rather than through desegregation. He brought national attention to the issues of urban education.

His solution rested on two tracks: identify the academically talented and train them to exercise creativity and leadership; and defuse the social dynamite with the promise of jobs through vocational education. Rather than reviewing the fabric of society itself, Conant remained focused on the outcomes of education.

Throughout his life Conant believed in the importance of education to transform an academically talented individual's life. Talent combined with schooling offered the keys of opportunity to the individual and creativity to the nation.

His vision of a comprehensive high school became the dominant model of education in the late 1950s and early 1960s, leading to the school consolidation movement and the regional high school. However, this did not serve the needs of the economically and socially deprived. Nevertheless, he was an important factor in bringing urban issues to the forefront of the national debate on education.

Great expectations and great teaching equals achievement. Let's take a lesson from Jaime Escalante. Garfield High School, a block from the hamburger-burrito stands, body shops and bars of Atlantic Boulevard in East Los Angeles, offered the worst possible conditions for learning (low-income, parents were grade-school dropouts, low faculty morale, low expectations).

Enter Jaime Escalante and his view that impoverished children can achieve as much as affluent kids if they are given enough extra study time and encouragement to learn. The idea that the sons and daughters of immigrant day laborers and seamstresses could be made to comprehend calculus, the intellectual triumph of Isaac Newton and Gottfried Leibnez, made no sense to anyone.

Escalante's students and other high poverty schools pulled it off. These schools simply had high expectations for every student. They arranged extra time for study after school, on Saturdays, and in summers and created a team spirit where teachers and students were working together to beat the big exam, the Advanced Placement Calculus AB exam.

Escalante celebrated "ganas," a Spanish word that he said meant "the urge to succeed." He was so convinced of the power of teaching that he lied to keep students with him. He said school rules forbade dropping his class. He told the parents of absent students that if he did not see their children in his classroom the next day, he would call the immigration authorities to check on their status.

Since the late 1980s and 1990s, schools like Garfield are emerging all over the country. Those schools are full of educators who have read everything they can find about Escalante. Kipp Schools have adopted his belief. It is amazing what teachers can do if they believe in their kids.

Escalante died in April 2010, still believing that great expectations and great teaching can equal achievement for all students.

Diane Ravitch is the nation's most vocal education historian. She once was one of the leading intellects behind the educational reform movement, emphasizing charter schools, testing, and accountability. Over the past few years she has become that movement's most vehement critic.

Ravitch pours out books, op-ed essays, and speeches. She is very forceful. She is quick to accuse people who disagree with her of being frauds and "greedheads." She picks and chooses what studies to cite. She has come to adopt the party-line view of the most change-averse elements of the teachers' unions: there is no educational crisis; poverty is the real issue, not bad schools. We don't need fundamental reform; we mainly need to give teachers more money and job security.

Many policy makers and educators say she is right. Teaching is a humane art built upon loving relationships between teachers and students. If you orient the system around a series of multiple choice accountability assessments, you distort it. If you make tests all-important you give schools an incentive to drop the subjects that don't show up on the exams. You may end up with schools that emphasize test taking, not genuine learning.

In sum, Ravitch highlights a core tension. Teaching is humane. Testing is mechanistic. Many educators agree with Ravitch and her narrative saying that America has humane local schools that are being threatened by testing wonks. Educators now are asking: Is the answer to keep the tests and the accountability, making sure every school has a clear sense of mission and invigorating moral culture, or do we continue teaching to the test?

Bill Gates continues to be a huge influence on education policy. Warren Buffet says every American, including himself, is lucky to have been born here. He calls us winners of the "ovarian lottery." But even within the United States, there is a huge gap between people who get the chance to make the most of their talents and those who don't. Bill and Melinda Gates believe that providing everyone with a great education is the key to closing this gap.

Gates stresses that to make a difference in a student's life we must have teachers that fuel interests and encourage students to read and learn as much as they can. Without these teachers students would never get on the path to become deeply engaged in learning.

The Gates Foundation decided in 2000 to invest in helping create better high schools. The goal was to give select schools extra money for a period of time to make changes in the way they were organized (including their size), in how teachers worked, and in their curriculum.

What Gates discovered was that many of the small schools he invested in did not improve student achievement in any significant way. These schools did not change their culture. Gates also discovered that some of the schools did achieve amazing things. These schools were charter schools. He visited High Tech High in San Diego and KIPP in Houston. These schools aimed high and embraced change. A great teacher became the key focal point.

In the future the Gates Foundation will focus on learning why some teachers are so much more effective than others and how best practices can be spread throughout the education system so the average quality goes up. Gates wants to replicate the models that work the best.

We dare not exclude the vision seekers. When people talk about schools, the word "vision" crops up again and again. Schools bring in experts to lead the school community through "visioning" sessions. These experts spout platitudes about how all students can learn. Futurists envision learning centers open twenty hours a day, with learning on demand by computer, etc. Some realize that any vision should mix with the here and now. A vision, to be useful, has to lead us from here to there.

Visionaries claim to believe in the importance of education as a national goal. Our self-image of American society as a learning society and of ourselves as number one in education as well as our rhetoric about life-long learning all support the value and meaning that education has for us as a society. Our very identity as Americans is based on our notions of freedom and democracy, which we know can be sustained only if our citizens are well educated. We need to envision all our schools as places dedicated to learning.

We are still faced with the question of who influences education in America. However, the question is impossible to answer because Americans are hopelessly ambivalent and often totally confused about what they want from their schools. Do we want a meritocracy with tough, unforgiving standards, or a democracy with endless second chances?

Do we want schools to prepare students to be effective economic competitors and reliable workers for employers, or to socialize kids and make them happy, well-adjusted individuals? Should they all be academically prepared for college? How many Americans want their kids to be intellectually engaged rather than popular with their peers?

What about daily prayer and Bible reading? In a democracy, when a majority of local voters want creation science to be taught, should this prevail? What about the teaching of contraception in sex-ed classes? Should community wishes or professional judgment prevail in the choice and exclusion of library books?

Unlike most of the other places we purport to envy for their academically successful education systems, currently Finland, Shanghai, and Korea, we don't have, or apparently even want, a single system—not a unified national system, anyway.

Currently the object of our envy is changing. A half century ago it was the Soviet Union; in the early 1980s it was Germany and Japan. In a culture like ours how could any individual voice or set of ideas or practices remain dominant or widely influential for any length of time?

The hottest thing a decade ago, No Child Left Behind set goals from day one that a lot of people knew were impossible to achieve. Now we are only trying to figure out how we can gracefully abandon them. It is a little like Afghanistan.

Educators say we are extinguishing creativity and the love of learning. Many believe that they are far higher predictors of achievement than current practices. It is sad that many of our policy makers are so shortsighted that they don't see the critical importance of intrinsic motivation and creative expression as the true drivers of productivity and innovation.

Competent, compliant workers do not create new economic avenues or advantages; these endeavors require too much time and effort for the uninspired to contribute significantly. Only people who are motivated by inner drive will invest (and risk) their lives and livelihoods in new ventures, which often have uncertain outcomes.

Unfortunately, the current mood in education is for external drivers to push students towards minimal proficiencies that can be measured by test scores. We are killing the intrinsic motivation to learn in most students who come through our educational system.

We need individuals who will stand for intrinsic motivation and creative expression that drive innovation and productivity and will fund public education based on them, instead of caving in to a narrow, dead-end business model of distance learning, large class size, more testing, more accountability, and the inevitable corollary, more cheating.

We need to address the lack of agreement about what constitutes learning and a good education. That is the crux of the matter. We have people who support: back to the basics, creative problem-solving, project-based learning, the lecture method, learning the dead-white-men classics, ignoring the classics, learning foreign languages, not bothering to learn one's native language, value-added evaluations, portfolio evaluations, standardized assessment, no standardized assessments, uniforms, no uniforms, restorative justice, conventional discipline, and the list goes on and on and on and on.

Some of these things can exist with others, but they can't all coexist. And yet many traditionalists insist on shoehorning every student into a single monopoly district whose fiefdom happens to cover the address where he or she lives.

Our world is becoming more diverse in almost every dimension and choices are multiplying everywhere. Our system needs to let go of the geographically defined, one-size-fits-all monopoly. Parents and students are demanding more and more choice in education that taxpayers provide. Unless educators address that fact, no individual will have any lasting influence on how our children learn.

Having said the above, we need to take action. Let's work together to give our kids good schools. Let's build a constituency of Americans who learn, vote, and act on behalf of quality public education.

State and local policy makers and educators make complex decisions that affect billions of public dollars and millions of school children. Policy makers today want high-quality, object-driven research to help guide their decisions.

Research can help only if based on the right questions. What is the relationship between education funding and student performance? How can we get the best return on our educational investment? How do schools achieve meaningful accountability? Do we need to revise governance arrangements? How do we connect policy and classroom change? How do we prepare teachers to implement reform?

The issue of bridging the gap between policy and practice has taken on greater importance. The adoption of reform creates expectations that changes will occur. Decision makers realize that they cannot make major changes without strong support from the citizenry. There is an emerging consensus that school reform must be a community-wide enterprise, carried out through partnerships with parents, businesses, social service agencies, and other institutions.

Restoring public confidence in public education is a major challenge in an era when a minority of the voting public has children in school and more parents are looking for choice alternatives for quality education. Policy makers and educators realize that to restore citizen confidence, they must make significant improvements in public education.

Improving education presents its own set of public challenges. Although many citizens support educational reform in general, they often disagree on the specifics or may be unprepared to accept the costs, discomfort, and timelines required to make significant changes.

Demographics and social changes are creating new governance, finance, and management challenges for education. Schools are enrolling more diverse students than ever before (limited English proficiency, varying ethnic and racial backgrounds). Social problems such as poverty, drugs, and crime are affecting children's health, safety, and readiness to learn.

Policy makers and educators also would like information about how to link K–12 education with learning before kindergarten and after high school. The increasing numbers of children with working parents or single parents, as well as the growing body of research about the importance of child development have heightened demands for quality early childhood services. Concerns among the business community about inadequately prepared high school graduates are causing educators and policy makers to rethink their school-to-work transition strategies.

Research is necessary to guide educators and policy makers in their decisions about new reforms, monitor the effects of current initiatives, and abolish ineffective programs. We must address the issues and questions the decision makers really care about. Information must be presented at the right time and in the right form to influence a policy audience.

How do we know if the research warrants policy changes? We begin by assessing the research and deciding how the research should be used. Next we look at the quality of the research. Is it valid, connected to prior research, ethical, and peer reviewed?

Further things to look at with regard to research warranting policy changes are the setting (urban studies may not fit rural areas), participants (ethnic students of color versus white), and the comparability of the program. In the end, research is a matter of balancing all the criteria of usefulness in a way that reflects the local circumstances involved in a particular policy decision.

To help communities achieve good schools policy makers firmly believe that public engagement plus specific school reform goals (based on research) lead to sustained policy, practice, and public responsibility. Engaging the public in school reform includes: community dialogue, building constituency, practitioners who are engaged, collaborating with other districts, policy analysis, legal strategies, and youth engagement.

All of the above is designed to build community accountability so that all children have the support they need to meet high standards of achievement. We need greater community responsibility for making sure all children, especially those on the margins, achieve at high levels.

Children need to enter school ready to learn, have access to a rich curriculum, receive quality instruction, and have access to community services that support and enhance learning. We must all work together and adopt action plans for educational policies that improve student achievement and also include a demand for quality public schools.

Can anyone influence education? Ponder the words of Rabindranath Tagore who wrote in "Gitanjali 35":

Where the mind is without fear and the head is held high;
Where knowledge is free;
Where the world has not been broken up into fragments by narrow domestic walls;
Whose words come out from the depth of truth;
Where tireless striving stretches its arms toward perfection;
Where the clear stream of reason has not lost its way into the dreary desert sand of dead habit;
Where the mind is led forward to ever-widening thought and action;
Into that heaven of freedom, let my country awake.

POINTS TO REMEMBER

- James Conant believed in the importance of education to transform student life.
- Jamie Escalante believed great expectations and great teaching equals achievement.
- Diane Ravitch is the educational reform movement's most vehement critic.
- Bill Gates says that good teachers make all the difference.
- There is lack of agreement about what constitutes learning and a good education.
- We must engage the public in influencing school reform.

Chapter Nine

New Trends in Education

Competition, Unemployment, Digital Devices and American Education

Nothing, not all the armies in the world can stop an idea whose time has come.
—Victor Hugo

Taking time to examine the strengths of the American educational system helps to put our myriad problems in perspective. There is no evidence that abandoning our public educational system will improve the situation. The strengths of the American educational system are embedded in our culture and history, and we should not discard them easily without better data about what works.

We need to consider the unique diversity of the American student body and the magnitude of demographic changes that are underway and what is yet to come.

We have not really been a "nation of nations" as both Carl Sandberg and Walt Whitman proclaimed. Rather, up until forty years ago, we have been a nation of Europeans. There was a common European culture that schools could use in socializing millions of immigrant children. Today we face a brand-new challenge: the population of American schools today truly represents the world. Children come to school with different diets, different music, and different languages.

The most diverse segment of our society is our children. They bring new energy and talents to our nation. They also represent new challenges for instruction. We must be willing to explore new trends in education that will give our children and young adults a sense of their own accomplishment in a supportive and enthusiastic environment.

Competition, Unemployment, Digital Devices, and American Education is a good theme to mention. For many the most frightening news in the last couple of months of 2010 was not North Korea stepping up its nuclear program, but an article about how American kids are stepping up their use of digital devices.

Look at the following scenario: Allison, age fourteen, sends and receives twenty-seven thousand texts in a month, her fingers clicking at a blistering pace as she carries on as many as seven text conversations at a time. She texts between classes, at the moment soccer practice ends, while on the bus to and from school, and often while doing homework.

This proficiency comes at a cost. She blames multitasking for the three Ds on her report card. "I'll be reading a book for homework and I'll get a text message and pause in my reading and put down the book, pick up the phone to reply to the text message, and then twenty minutes later realize I forgot to do my homework."

Texting is an issue integral to a larger problem. Academics are faltering and this leads to unemployment. Our unemployment today is not only because of the financial crisis. There are some deeper problems. If we're going to get more Americans back to work we need to get help from the government, from the top down and we also need more stimulus from educators, from the bottom up.

The deeper problems fostering unemployment in America today can be summarized in three paragraphs:

Global competition is stiffer. Just think about two of our most elite colleges. When Harvard and Yale were all male, applicants had to compete only against a pool of white males to get in. But when Harvard and Yale admitted women and more minorities, white males had to step up their game.

When the cold war ended, globalization took hold. As Harvard and Yale started to admit more Chinese, Indian, Singaporean, Polish, and Vietnamese students, both American men and women had to step up their games to get in. And as the educational systems of China, India, Singapore, Poland, and Vietnam continue to improve, and more of their cream rises to the top and more young people apply to Ivy League schools, it is only going to get more competitive for American men and women at every school.

Then, just as the world started getting flattened by globalization, technology went on a rampage, destroying more low-end jobs and creating more high-end jobs faster than ever. What computers, hand-held devices, wireless technology, and robots do in aggregate is empower better educated and higher skilled workers to be more productive, so they can raise their incomes, while eliminating many lower-skilled service and factory jobs altogether.

Now the best-educated workers, capable of doing the critical thinking that machines can't do, get richer while the least educated get pink slips. In many businesses, receptionists are replaced by a microchip and the employees get voice mail.

Finally, just when globalization and technology were making the value of higher education greater than ever, and the price for lacking it more punishing than ever, America started slipping behind its peers in high school graduation rates, college graduation rates, and global test scores in math and critical thinking.

Education secretary Arnie Duncan says that fifty years ago if you dropped out, you could get a job in the stockyards or the steel mills and still be able to own your home and support your family. Today there are no such jobs for high school dropouts. Duncan goes on to say that they are gone and Americans have not adjusted to this.

Many believe that when kids drop out today they are condemned to poverty and social failure. There are barely any jobs left for someone with only a high school diploma. This diploma is only valuable today if it has truly prepared you to go on to higher education. This is your ticket to a decent job.

Beyond the recession, this triple whammy is one of the main reasons that middle-class wages have been stagnating. To overcome that we need teachers and principals who are paid better for better performance, but also valued for their long hours and dedication to students and learning. We need parents ready to hold their kids to higher standards of academic achievement. We need students who come to school ready to learn, not text. To support all of this we need an all-society effort, from the White House to the classroom to the living room.

If you want to know who is doing the parenting part correctly, start with the immigrants who know that learning is the way up. Over half of the thirty-two winners of Rhodes Scholarships for 2011 (America's top college graduates) have names like Mark Jai, Aakash Shah, Zeijaja Taugeer, Tracy Yang, Baltazar Zavala, Prerna Nadathur, Renugan Raidoo, and so on. Do you see the picture?

Technology: is it oversold and underused? We have to keep ahead of the global economy. The best schools have the most sophisticated computers. Our kids can't be left behind. Our kids need the best.

For the past twenty years, many educators, public officials, and business leaders have argued that to keep ahead, American children need to be computer savvy from early childhood onward. Using computers and the Internet in school will give kids a huge academic advantage and in the long run, prepare them to be winners in an ever more competitive workplace. In fact real-estate agents and parents cite the number of computers in their child's school to demonstrate the quality of the education offered. Computers and technology are a trend and can be useful when teachers understand and believe in their power to enhance student learning.

One way that some policy makers advocate computers and technology be used is in learning a language. There is an evolution of language learning online. Collaborative learning is happening online where students tutor one another. Here is a scenario from an expert encountered on the web: The message from the seventeen-year-old Tunisian skateboarder was curt. "Totally wrong," he said of my French. My conjugation was off and I should study spelling. On a scale of one to five, the skateboarder said that my French practice essay was worth a one. Then he disappeared into the anonymity of the Internet.

As my young Tunisian tutor was showing me, the Internet, with its unparalleled ability to connect people throughout the world, is changing the way we can learn a language. There is still no way to avoid the hard slog through vocabulary lists and grammar rules, but the books, tapes, and CDs of yesteryear are being replaced by e-mail, video chats, and social networks.

Livemocha.com is a Seattle company with millions in venture capital financing that mixes social network with lessons for more than thirty-eight of the world's most common languages. The initial lessons are free (a charge comes later for more advanced lessons) or you can agree to correct the work of others, something my friend in Tunisia was doing for me.

The casual connections with real people throughout the world, however brief, are not just for fun. They reveal how the language is really used. You learn something about slang and attitude rarely found in books.

Livemocha.com is experimenting with a variety of ways to motivate people that resemble the social games found on Facebook. The language programs have each person set up a profile that includes a short description of age, location, and what you would like to talk about. You then find the right person through what are essentially classified ads. If you want to study Luxembourgish, the Germanic language of Luxembourg, you find eleven people there looking to study English who are willing to teach the language. There are thirty-two willing people who are fluent in Tswana, a Bantu language spoken around South Africa, namely in Botswana. All that it takes to find a study partner is one e-mail or two.

Is this a new educational trend that can be used in your school? You decide.

Problem, project, and inquiry-based learning are trends being adopted by many school districts across America. All three closely relate to the information-processing approach. They all fit well with the technology-rich learning environments where the focus is not on the hardware or software, but on the learning experience.

In each case, technology is used to facilitate leaning. It may be a tool to organize ideas (inspiration), search for current information (online news source), or present ideas (PowerPoint). However, the focus of the learning environment is the students' excitement about solving a problem or addressing a meaningful issue. It is simply a process of problem solving and acquiring knowledge.

Learning is made relevant and useful, and provides opportunities for teachers to build relationships. Student work is shared with other teachers, parents, and the business community, all of whom have a stake in the students' education.

Technology has become a popular tool in project, problem, and inquiry-based learning. Students use web resources, electronic databases, and e-mail. No longer are products restricted to term papers or posters. Students are creating videos and are being published on the web.

When we think about "best" approach we consider the one that works for you in your classroom. Many teachers have chosen to blend project, problem, and inquiry-based learning together. Others may use them separately. The choice is yours.

The strengths movement in America's schools is catching on. A consortium of like-minded educators, parents, health providers, career counselors, and social service agencies have come together to bring schools, businesses, and community leaders across the United States to form a grassroots coalition to push for legislation that mandates schools focus on developing students' strengths.

Jennifer Fox, director of the Purnell School in Pottersville, New Jersey, has developed the Affinities Program. This is a four-year curriculum designed to help students understand what they feel most energized doing. What are a student's strengths? The Affinities Program is an original, organic approach for young people to develop their strengths using hands-on interdisciplinary activities. Fox is convinced that America's schools need to stop the sole focus on remediation of weakness and standardized tests at the expense of nurturing a child's passion.

Fox believes the time for change is now. If student accountability can be a government mandate, so can programming to help students discover their unique strengths. She is also appealing to business leaders to push the movement forward because their future employees will come, whether they are prepared to contribute their strengths or are deflated by overemphasis on their weaknesses. She believes that we can give so much more and get so much more as a society if we switch the focus to developing and identifying strengths.

How about remixing education with the hip-hop pedagogy. The following information is taken from an interview with Sam Seidel in 2009. Sam Seidel and his colleagues use the term "Hip Hop Genius," by which he means creative resourcefulness in the face of limited resources. When he uses the term hip-hop he is not just talking about music. He is referring to the unique blend of instincts, confidence, and ingenuity that develops in oppressed communities as has been demonstrated through the evolution of hip-hop culture.

Faced with racism, classism, ageism, and other forms of structural subjugations, instead of breaking down and giving in to stereotypes and statistics, young people have developed new forms of art and businesses as well as believing they can do something that's never been done. This is hip-hop genius.

Many educators view hip-hop as a negative influence in students' lives. Teachers are concerned that hip-hop music promotes violence, misogyny, homophobia, hyper-capitalistic consumption, and bad grammar. Hip-hop is seen as a force that competes for students' attention, which frustrates teachers attempting to engage students, only to be drowned out by cultural products that often critique the very voices schools are trying to instill.

Layers of racism, classism, and ageism all factor into educators' frustration with a medium created by young black and Latino people from low-income communities, a medium that is widely successful in engaging the very students schools struggle to reach.

How can we embrace and embody innovative instincts in the field of education? Under the hip-hop pedagogy, students learn through independent projects, which allow students to play an active role in their education and demonstrate confidence in their ability to take responsibility for themselves. Hip-hop took classical dance, flipped it on its head and literally spun it around.

Students are learning through partnerships with business and public entities. Students start and cross-promote their own record labels, media outlets, clothing brands, fragrances, and beverage companies following the lead of hip-hop artists who have crafted a fresh approach to the art of business. They create their own music while learning about the music business through workshops.

Hip-hop educators embrace the spirit of entrepreneurial collaboration to provide their students with valuable opportunities for authentic work experiences, career exploration, and engaging connections to academic content.

Respecting students means not only embracing music and culture, but also working hard to cultivate conditions that honor their realities and foster success. Hip-hop schools have gone to great lengths to understand the problem of attendance and to generate innovative solutions. Schools start at 10 a.m. and remain open until 8 p.m. Given that most arrests of teenagers occur during weekday afternoons, keeping schools open during these times helps students stay productive and avoid dangerous situations.

This is hip-hop genius. Many educators say that we need more of it. We need thirsty young hustlers ready to remix the education equation. We should not only alter the content of traditional instruction, but also build environments that are more responsive to young people's ingenuity, interests, and needs.

Sam Seidel and colleagues urge the creating of schools that not only teach hip-hop, but are hip-hop.

Facebook is a huge trend facing our schools and we need to reconcile ourselves with it. Students are addicted to Facebook. You see it with students who put it well ahead of academics. Schools need to face the fact that the extent of this technology is huge. This new media is changing education. People are dependent on social networking. Many teachers are now using Facebook in a positive way as they contact students regarding attendance, graduation, assignments, and grades.

Another trend that the schools are considering in many areas across the nation is the end of homework. One group of educators firmly believes that homework disrupts families, over-burdens children, and even limits learning.

In 1901, homework was legally banned in California. By 1960 assigning homework to our children carried a priority equal to national security. Recent years show that, ten years into the twenty-first century, American schools have steadily increased the number of hours of work expected of students after school. The bone crushing backpacks American children shoulder home nightly is evidence of the burden attributed to homework.

A growing number of educators feel that homework is a great discriminator. Some children go home to computers, libraries, and well-educated parents. Others have challenging home environments, after-school jobs, and family responsibilities. Schools need to ensure equal opportunities for educational advancement, to offer resources to all children, and not to privilege inadvertently any one group of students.

Consider these scenarios: A fifth grader comes home in tears nightly; she has so much homework she can't play in the soccer league anymore. A third-grade teacher admonishes parents that homework needs to take priority over outside music lessons and religious education.

The scenarios continue. A father of a seventh grader gives away his season tickets to the local basketball team because his son can't take a night off from homework during the week. An eighth grader finds she is at the bottom of her class, despite her best efforts because she doesn't have a computer at home and can't keep up with her peers who do.

Every night, around thousands of kitchen tables, the homework wars erupt, as parents try to rescue some semblance of family life from the demands of homework. Is there no escape from the tyranny of homework?

Would American students fall behind in the global village if homework were cut back? Are schools using homework as a way to extend the demands of schools without extending school hours?

Let's look at homework in the historical perspective. During the nineteenth century education focused on reading, writing, and math and when students reached fifth grade large numbers left for work. By the late nineteenth century a majority of Americans had migrated to the city and, due to long hours in the factories, family life deteriorated.

During the first half of the twentieth century educators were more concerned with health and happiness and that homework would be an intrusion into family life and interfere with the rights of both children and parents. Physicians joined the battle citing the health risks of homework. For instance, acne was the direct cause of lack of fresh air and sunshine due to homework.

Homework faded away until the 1957 launch of *Sputnik*. The Russians "beat" us into space and permanently damaged the American educational landscape. The fifty-year trend of less or no homework came to a screeching halt. The country became obsessed with competing with the Russians. Homework became the primary means of increasing academic achievement.

As the United States entered the 1980s, education reform became a key item with the publishing of *A Nation at Risk*. Homework was on center stage again and by 1990 politicians were demanding Congress to mandate more and more homework. The amount of homework has risen ever since.

Why don't students do their homework? They just don't have enough time, they have family responsibilities, and there is no point in doing it because teachers do not collect it or it had nothing to do with what they were being tested on. For many students homework is more of a hindrance than a help.

Sally, sixteen, says, "It is hard to do homework when you have a baby to take care of."

Matt, fifteen, says, "I did my homework but forgot to have my parents sign it so I forged the signatures because my parents work at night. The teacher knew it, threw away my homework, and gave me a detention."

Tray, seventeen, says, "I knew I wasn't going to make it my junior year. I lasted two months, fell behind in my homework, couldn't catch up, and failed my classes. I dropped out after that."

Demetrius, sixteen, says, "The teacher called me worthless because I did not complete my homework. I just don't do anything any more."

These comments raise all sorts of questions that we rarely think about. When students say they can't finish their homework, why do teachers assume they are lying? Did anyone bother to ask why?

The bottom line is that although homework causes much anguish in many homes, not only for children but also for parents, it is one of the most entrenched institutional practices in American education. Despite periodic attempts to lighten the load or redistribute the burden, few efforts to reform homework have met with success.

The final trend worth looking at is the single parent. A single parent is defined as a parent who cares for one or more children without the assistance of another parent in the home. Single parenthood occurs for a variety of reasons (divorce, adoption, artificial insemination, extra-marital pregnancy, death, or abandonment).

One thing to remember is that single parenthood is a stage of life, rather than a life-long family form. Many re-partner and form step families. According to Families and Living Arrangements (2010) there were 13.9 million one-parent families in the nation; 11.4 million were single-mothers families and 2.5 million single-father families. This data come from the 2010 Current Population Surveys and the Annual Social and Economic Supplement conducted in February, March, and April.

Single-parent families are at risk for poverty and poor health. There is concern for increased risk of negative social, behavioral, and emotional outcomes for children. Factors that influence how children develop in single-parent homes are parental age, level of education, occupation (if any), income (if any), and the parent's support network of friends and extended family.

Single parents have often been the focus of public policy debate. What is the role of government in their support? Morally, how does the decline of the traditional family affect us? Liberal educators welcome changes in family structures; conservative educators decry the decline of marriage, rise of divorce, and cohabitation. Schools are caught in the middle.

There are impacts of sole parenting on children, and educators need to become more aware of the emotional, social, behavioral, and academic outcomes of this more acceptable way of life.

The success of the teaching/learning dynamic rests with both the learner and the teacher. We all must make good judgments that set the stage for success. Change often involves giving up something. We need to be ready to add new ideas and stretch old ones. It also involves replacing ideas—replacing our old images and conceptions with new images of aims, outcomes, and methods.

Looking at current, new, and even past trends forces us to ask questions and then proceed according to answers that are developing. The questions are significant. How is learning self-regulated? What is knowledge? How do we perceive families, students, and environments?

Schools must focus on helping learners create new knowledge by helping them cope with new rules, laws, constraints, and realities.

We must look at trends carefully. Schools are for learners already living a life, not preparing to live a life. The lives they are presently living must be honored. Let's reclaim the essence of learning.

POINTS TO REMEMBER

- The relationship between competition, unemployment, digital devices, and American education is a current issue.
- Livemocha.com is a revolutionary way to use the Internet to teach languages.
- Problem, project, and inquiry-based learning are trends being adopted across American schools.
- The strengths movement is overcoming negativity.
- Hip-hop pedagogy is altering traditional instruction.
- The issue of homework is grounds for reform.
- We must become more aware of the emotional, social, behavioral, and academic outcomes due to the new trend of single parenthood.

Chapter Ten

Future Trends in Education

Why Study the Future?

The real voyage of discovery lies not in seeking new landscapes, but in having new eyes. —Marcel Proust

Education is not an island; it is affected not only by what is happening in the field, but also by what is happening in the rest of society: population changes, technological advances, economic ups and downs, political shifts, and social transformations.

We must focus on examining ongoing and emerging trends and explore how these trends may affect education in the United States over the next twenty to thirty years. Examining trends allows organizations to anticipate change, rather than react to it. Trends do *not* predict what the future will be, but rather indicate directions of change and bring focus to what the future may look like.

Futurists have identified dozens of long-term trends that define and constrain the way Americans conceive the future. Why then study the future? The world changes so quickly it's hard to keep up. New inventions and innovations alter the way we live. People's values, attitudes, and beliefs are changing. The pace of change keeps accelerating, making it difficult to prepare for tomorrow.

By studying the future, people can better anticipate what lies ahead. More importantly, they can actively decide how they will live in the future, by making choices today and realizing the consequences of their decisions. The future doesn't just happen. People create it through their action, or inaction, today.

No one knows exactly what will happen in the future. But by considering what might happen, people can more rationally decide on the sort of future that would be most desirable and then work to achieve it. Opportunity as well as danger lies ahead, so people need to make farsighted decisions. The process of change is inevitable. It's up to everyone to make sure that the change is constructive.

The world is changing in ways that dramatically alter the assumptions, beliefs, traditions, and policies that previously served American citizens. Moreover, the rate of change is increasing at an astounding pace, resulting in many traditions and institutions lagging behind developments in some areas, such as technology. As stated earlier, to anticipate change, rather than react to it, organizations are identifying trends and examining their possible implications. These trends are so pervasive or self-evident as to be invisible, much like water is to fish.

What follows are some broad trends likely to affect education, directly or indirectly. We have increasing dominance of technology in the economy and society, expanding education throughout society and lifetimes, and a declining middle-class with a widening gap between the "haves" and the "have nots."

We see an increase in metropolitanization/suburbanization, a rise of knowledge industries and knowledge-dependent society, with an increasingly global economy. There is a shift in the traditional nuclear family to more single-parent families. Finally, there are growing demands for accountability in use of public funds.

First, focus on educational trends. The context within which American children are schooled has been evolving for some time now. Educational reform occurs in cycles, and policy makers, educators and citizens are in the midst of a long-standing quest for improving the quality of education. The "solution" may be the panoply of approaches and experiments. At one time, what was taught and how it was taught varied little across the country, but today a number of educational approaches are available.

This evolution reflects the context in which future trends will play out in education. We are moving from certain things toward certain things. One should not always replace the other but move toward balance between the two.

We are moving from high compliance toward high achievement, time-driven to results-driven, and subject knowledge to process knowledge (learning to learn). We are also moving from rote learning to critical thinking and from focusing on academic weakness toward focusing on academic strengths.

New developments in education technology, from Internet access to new teaching techniques enabled by classroom computers, are also driving changes in the educational environment. The trend is from school-time learning toward learning anytime, or anyplace, from teacher-centered toward student-centered classrooms, and from textbook funds to educational resource funds.

The key trends within education now and in the foreseeable future concern increases in school competition, accountability, contracting for services, and demand for quality educators. These trends and their possible implications for education are addressed below.

Competition among schools for students, educators, and funds is increasing. The watchword for the future in public education is choice. Charter schools, magnet schools, homeschooling, vouchers, and contract education providers point to the proliferation of school choice, which is driving competition for students and teachers. Some proponents see the advent of choices for K–12 schooling as the salvation of the nation's educational system; some opponents see it as the system's final undoing. However one looks at it, the public education monopoly is being challenged.

Some possible outcomes from the increasing competition are: student achievement levels may rise and teacher performance may improve as schools jockey for a better position in the marketplace. A more competitive educational environment may attract a higher caliber of professionals to teacher and administrative positions. On the other hand, public schools may be stripped of their best students, leaving the poor, disadvantaged, and special needs students behind.

Calls for education accountability are increasing at all levels. The factory model of schooling exemplified by a one-size-fits-all, advancing-through-grades-in-a-lockstep approach has given way to a model based on standards and testing for competency. How students acquire skills and knowledge is less important than their ability to meet certain competency standards. Furthermore, the emphasis is shifting to applying academic study toward practical outcomes, such as communicating effectively, solving problems, and thinking critically.

Just as doing "seat time" will no longer guarantee students a diploma, educators and administrators are being held accountable for the outcomes of their work. Also, as new evidence of instructional techniques that shatter the barriers of race and socioeconomic status comes to light, schools with disadvantaged and students of color will stand to gain. Those that fail to meet expectations will face consequences, which many include denial of a diploma for failing students, school closure for low-performing schools, or state or city takeover of low-performing districts.

The implications include states demanding better data collection and more sophisticated use of information technology. Demand is likely to increase for solid educational policy research about what works to improve teaching and learning.

Colleges of education may be held accountable for teacher quality. The disconnect between institutions of higher education and the P–12 system will wane, as calls for comprehensive, seamless educational systems grow stronger.

Finally, long-standing ideas about academic ability and prospects of students from disadvantaged communities are changing. Schools and districts serving these populations can no longer shrug off poor student performance as inevitable.

More school districts and states are contracting for educational services. The quest for accountability and frustration with a seemingly intractable bureaucracy have made the notion of contracting for services much more attractive. Colleges, nonprofits and for-profit companies are managing newly created public schools or taking over poorly performing schools in several states.

The advent of contract providers for educational services gives decision makers a new and powerful item in the school improvement toolbox. Implications of this trend include: educational governing bodies may serve as procurers, rather than direct providers of services. Persons who serve in administrative positions, on school boards, and in statewide offices may need new or different skills to succeed. Management or legal skills may assume more importance. Innovators may have the edge over keepers of the status quo.

The demand for educational professionals is rising. With a large portion of the education workforce due to retire in the coming decade, coupled with a boom in school-age children, the demand for teachers, substitutes, principals, and other educators will be significant.

The implications of this trend include: the "monopoly" on teacher certification will come to an end. Alternative methods of teacher certification may be needed to meet the growing demand for qualified teachers. Educators and professionals in other fields may have more career options available to them.

Future schools may attract people with different qualifications and backgrounds to education. Teacher training is likely to change according to new standards and methodologies. The educational bureaucracy, which for decades seemed impervious to reform efforts, may undergo even more transformation as new workers and leaders trained in the emerging climate of accountability and school choice assume control.

The next focus is on demographic trends. Franklin D. Roosevelt said (in 1936), "To some generations, much is given. Of other generations much is expected. This generation has a rendezvous with destiny." Demographics become destiny as the baby boom generation illustrates so vividly. Data will tell us a great deal about upcoming student populations, from their socioeconomic status to how many seats they will fill in tomorrow's classrooms.

In a time of rapid change and increasing uncertainty, demographic data provide the most reliable source of information about what the future may bring. Examining demographic data related to race, phase of life, ethnicity, age, and poverty provides information about what the American student population will look like in the next ten to fifteen years.

"Minority" students are forming the student majority. While the birthrate for whites is declining, American population increases will be driven by high rates of immigration for Hispanic and new African students. The U.S. Census Bureau projects the majority of American school-age children will be members of a racial/ethnic minority by 2030; nearly one in four will likely be of Hispanic origin. Conversely, the percentage of minority teachers continues to dwindle.

The implications are that educators will have to accommodate the needs of a student population vastly different from those of previous years. Colleges of education must prepare teachers to instruct widely varying student populations. The demand for bilingual teachers and principals may surge. Educators and policy makers may have to invest considerable effort and resources in curtailing the current dropout rate among Hispanic, American Indian, and African American students.

School segregation is increasing. After decades of decline, studies show school segregation is again on the rise, particularly for Latino students. Immigration patterns and the reversal of desegregation rulings indicate this trend is likely to continue. Furthering this trend are the rise in schooling choices and the widening income gap between society's wealthiest and poorest populations. As noted previously, students in the upper socioeconomic strata may opt out of public schools, leaving low-income, non-English speaking students behind.

Implications that come to mind are: overt and covert racism, debate over bilingual education, polarization and prejudice, ballot initiatives from special interest and fringe groups, and disparate points of view concerning the necessary direction of the country, states, and localities.

Disproportionate numbers of children and women are filling the ranks of the poor. Given the likely reality of rising numbers of economically disadvantaged children from single-parent homes, educational policy makers will need to rethink the roles and priorities of public education institutions.

The implications arise in the form of questions. Will students in the future come to school less ready to learn than in the past? How will equitable educational opportunities be afforded to all students? How will resources best be allocated among academic, remedial, athletic, after-school, and school-to-work programs? Which curricula are most appropriate? Should students be prepared for jobs that may not exist or be given a liberal arts base from which to build?

The number of senior citizens is growing. In 2011, the first of the baby boomers turned sixty-five and seventy million people will follow suit by 2020. The "new" seniors are expected to be wealthier and more inclined to exercise political clout than their predecessors.

The implication here is that funding K–12 education will become more challenging as the population ages. School-age population growth will demand new buildings, updates, and expansions of older buildings. At the same time, older home owners may balk at footing the bill, thus forcing school districts to develop alternative funding formulas.

Technological trends are next in line. The history of civilization is largely defined by technological developments, from the simple mastery of fire to the complexity of space travel. Today, the defining factor driving change in nearly every sector of life is the digital revolution. In essence, computing devices are becoming smaller, cheaper, more powerful and more connected to one another.

If the history of technological advances is any guide, changes in education may be profound, complex, interrelated, delayed, and often unexpected. Educational technology proponents argue that not since the Gutenberg printing press made possible the printing of primers and textbooks has technological advancement possessed such potential to transform education.

Technology is increasingly being used to change what happens in the classroom or the school. Technology's most significant effects on education are likely to come from using it to solve seemingly intractable problems or to do things entirely differently. For example, teachers may be better able to take a more student-centered approach to learning and accommodate multiple learning styles. In addition, they will use new forms of communication (e-mail, texting, social networks, etc). This will increase parental involvement in schools; they will be able to track student progress more efficiently.

Economic trends are crucial. Although the state of the economy is beyond the district control of those charged with education governance, the economy strongly affects education. The globalization of the economy and near-instantaneous world communications make it difficult to chart a course for economic prosperity in the future. No one knows how national economics will perform now that national economic boundaries are increasingly blurred.

Wealth is becoming concentrated in a shrinking elite. Americans in the top 5 percent income bracket earn 13 times as much as those in the bottom 5 percent. The CEOs of the top 3,000 American companies earn 212 times what the average worker earns.

This concentration of wealth in a shrinking elite may have several implications for education: the upper class may opt for private schools, leaving public schools with a greater proportion of students arriving at school with unmet needs. The increasing percentage of minority students, many whom come from lower-income homes, is likely to place additional demands on school systems. The educational quality may vary widely across economic strata.

The unemployment rate does not reveal the extent of employment problems. While millions are officially unemployed, the U.S. Bureau of Labor Statistics and the U.S. Census Bureau estimate that additional millions are unemployed but uncounted. The implications are: if the unemployment count is increasing, the purpose of education may need to change. School funding formulas will need to be revised.

The demand for technically skilled workers is high. Jobs requiring technical skills, but not necessarily a college degree, will be in demand in the future. Changing economic conditions will warrant and/or trigger curricular changes resulting from changing work prospects. Will technical and vocational training gain or lose ground in the K–12 setting? What will become of school-to-work programs?

We can't forget about political trends. Political change in the United States fortunately takes place at a much slower pace than technological change or even economic change. In government and politics, stability is the name of the game, shifts in power between the two major parties notwithstanding. Internationally, the picture is less stable as shown by new political and economic alignments.

The call for public accountability is increasing as taxpayers question the spending habits and policies of representative government. The taxpayer revolt is strong. The aging baby boomers and their increasing reliance on a culturally and racially diverse population to fund their retirement years is resulting in political tensions that will erode the tax base and get progressively worse.

The distrust of the federal government is rising. The hardships of the underclass and economic disparities are driving forces behind a growing antigovernment movement. Fear of an uncertain future is driving more and more people from the mainstream to the margins of society, where they are seeking refuge in political and religious movements that promise to restore public order and put people back to work

Will there be declining purchasing power plaguing the global economy and undermining the capacity of governments to effectively manage their own affairs? Will homeschooling be the answer to education in the future? Will there be new demands for services in public schools?

Finally we look at social trends. The baby boomers are determined to provide a wholesome and protected environment for their offspring. They demand quality education.

Consumer behavior is becoming driven by the desire to self-differentiate. Consumers are developing a penchant for self-differentiation and nonconformity. Accordingly, mass marketing is giving way to niche marketing.

The urge to define one's self by the products and services consumed provides the backdrop for lifestyle choice, consumer behavior, political behavior, education choices, and expectations.

The implication to this is that providers of education, faced with growing competition for students, should sharpen marketing skills. Consumers will expect to see a school's performance record, areas of focus, and areas of teacher expertise before enrolling their children.

Nonprofit organizations are playing an increasingly important role in providing social services. Schools may be pressed into providing services or dealing with the consequences of inadequate services. More schools will partner with nonprofits to help students succeed in school.

New social ills are revealing the dark side of progress. The presence of disenfranchised, alienated youth is hardly a new phenomenon, but changing times are yielding new means for acting out antisocial or aggressive tendencies. Violence is increasing, rural America's pastoral image is being tarnished, and increasing access to virtual reality is leading to new kinds of maladies. Education will feel the effect as school safety becomes an issue for school and community leaders.

Trends do not continue indefinitely. Futurists speak of mature trends and emerging trends. A number of long-term trends are identified, such as increasing metropolitanization and suburbanization. These long-term trends form the backdrop for current developments and are widely recognized by the general public. We need to focus on the key emerging trends likely to affect education. Emerging trends can take a little more effort to detect. There are the ones that, with hindsight, decision makers say, "It was there all along. Why didn't we recognize that change?"

When situations move far enough afield from the norm or center, the change process rolls into motion. For example, a decline in urban school performance will be tolerated for only so long before parents, administrators, and other stakeholders band together and declare war on the problem.

In political cycles, popular ideology shifts, or as some say, "the center shifts," but the pendulum eventually swings. Hence, trend identification and analysis can be useful in generating a call to action, or, even better, can spur decision makers to identify a preferred future and chart a course for getting there.

As Jim Taylor and Watts Wacker said (in *The 500-Year Delta*), "The critical issue in planning today is not how to get there. The critical issue is where you want to be." Keep that in mind when you consider future trends in education and how they will affect the educational system in America.

POINTS TO REMEMBER

- Educational trends include competition, more accountability, contracting for services, and a demand for educational professionals.
- Demographic trends include minority students forming the majority, school segregation, children of poverty, and the increasing numbers of senior citizens.
- Technological trends are changing the classroom structure.
- Economic trends include wealth becoming concentrated in a shrinking elite, unemployment rising, demand for high tech workers increasing, and the distrust and spending of government being questioned.
- Social trends include consumer behavior being driven by self-differentiation and nonprofits providing more services to schools.

Chapter Eleven

Results Matter

The Key to Saving American Education

It is not our role to speak to the people about our own view of the world, nor to attempt to impose that view on them, but rather to dialogue with the people about their view and ours. —Professor Ho-Won Jeong

An old Jewish proverb goes something like this, "May you live in exciting times." This wish has certainly come to pass for our generation and for those of us engaged in education. But for many of us this could have a different look. From one angle, we see exciting opportunities for change. If we blink we might see the same image as a frightening roadblock.

Actions are important but the thinking that influences and shapes what we actually do is far more critical. Changing our thinking is the first step.

The journey to change has many opinions, perspectives, and visions, and we find we are having trouble communicating with each other about the best way to educate our children.

Everyone has an opinion about education. Newspapers, documentaries, teachers, administrators, business leaders, parents, and even students all voice their opinions and concerns. Despite the search for common viewpoints, multiple reforms, and lots of "what ifs," much stays the same. Our collective pictures and visions do not match even when we use common threads.

We might agree that all students need to master the basics. To a traditional educator you stress discipline and require students to sit in a desk and listen to the teacher. On the other hand, businesses with a futuristic bent might mean something different. They want people with self-discipline and enough basics to include fundamental reading, writing, and math. They want people who can take charge, be team players, be creative and innovative, and focus on possibilities, not just "right answers."

People hold different views on how information is delivered to students. Who controls the flow? What is the teacher's role in technology? If a computer can better teach facts and skills, what do teachers teach?

As educators we know technology alone will never be enough. Education serves to give a country a shared social fabric, a heritage deeply steeped in democratic principles.

How do we approach conflict and crisis in education? This approach hinges on how human beings learn. Only in America were the common folk of the Old World given a chance to show what they could do on their own, without a master to order them about. History contrived an earthshaking joke when it lifted up by the nape of the neck lowly peasants, shopkeepers, laborers, paupers, jailbirds, and drunks from the midst of Europe, dumped them on a vast virgin continent and said, "Go to it. It's yours!"

Children who are allowed to take responsibility and given a serious part in the larger world are always superior. Students are questioning traditional authority. From the Discovery Channel to the Internet, students are getting information and contradicting teachers. They voice the opinions of talk show hosts and are challenging some of our taken-for-granted value systems. Students see adults *not* practicing what they preach.

The bigger picture, of which chaos is a huge part, is the physical understanding of how order evolves, why change is inevitable in an educational system designed to be stable and resist change, and what factors underlie transformation. We are experiencing a shift in our own most fundamental assumptions.

Everyone engages in some type of self-reference. People will interpret the situation differently. Some will welcome change. Some will retreat and seek to barricade themselves. Some will confront change. All involved will interpret the situation in terms of their beliefs and values, their mental models of how the world and education should work.

The time has come for educators to rethink why we educate. Are students simply individuals who must ingest some form of the basics to survive, consume, and produce, or is education about helping children, who are capable of self-reflection and self-organization, and of enjoying a life where they explore their abundant potential? Is it education to enjoy listening to and playing music, or is it only education if we are taught about the mechanics of music?

We must remember that it is not our role to speak about our view of the world. We should not attempt to impose that view on students, but rather to dialogue about their views and ours.

Education is not carried on by "A" *for* "B" or by "A" *about* "B," but rather by "A" *with* "B," mediated by the world—a world, which impresses and challenges both parties, giving rise to views and opinions about it. You must be partners and in a relationship with each other.

We need to amplify the voices of practitioners, students, and partner organizations, so that the stories can come together and shape how policies are made and clarify what purpose they should have.

To do this more effectively, we need to hear from you. Together, let's make sure the lessons of the past aren't forgotten. Ensure that all young people acquire the skills and self-confidence they need to be seen and heard in meaningful, responsible ways.

The lessons of the past help students confront the necessity for responsible participation to promote democracy, justice, and human dignity in the future. It takes courage to be able to stand up for what you're doing and maybe take a hit sometimes. Have courage to act on your beliefs.

The twentieth century, for all its scientific and technological amazements, might be described as a century in which we watered down our own humanity. We turned wisdom into information, community into consumerism, politics into manipulation, and destiny into DNA.

Education has not been exempt from this process. Early in the century we took teaching and learning, that ancient exchange between student and teacher and the world and started thinning it down into little more than the amassing of data and the mastering of technique.

That is the bad news. The good news is that in the last few decades people saw right through it. Teachers, administrators, parents, and citizens who care about education have been working hard to reclaim the integrity of teaching and learning so that it can once again become a process in which the whole person is nourished.

America's legacy to its young people includes bad schools, poor health care, deadly addictions, crushing debts, and utter indifference. We are constantly grappling with the concept of courage and fear and violence, sacrifice and scapegoating, imitation and exposure.

As we examine American education we increasingly criticize our capacity to be strong, ethically, politically, socially, and economically. Do we even have a hope filled future?

We need a new direction in our national conversation about educational reform. Many of us who care about education are disheartened by the "fixes" put forward by our political leaders. They too often promote simplistic answers that attempt to change education from the outside in, such as establishing one-size-fits-all standards to which all students and teachers must measure up or be judged as failures.

If we can give our youth the tools they need, challenge them in constructive ways to let go and choose growth, perhaps the next generation will not always need to learn the "hard way."

Many adults have judged this generation of adolescents as shallow, selfish, and vacuous. The wisdom, wonder, and search of young people today often go unseen or misunderstood beneath all the defenses they have erected to protect their fragility and to express their despair. Those who recognize hunger in the voices of students may discover their own ways to respond to their needs.

Controversy and confusion can divide us, pitting us against one another and preventing us from taking action. Despite our differences let's come together to foster connection, meaning, and integrity. Honor our students to search for what *they* believe.

We can discourse all we want about what-ifs and what should be, but the bottom line is that results matter. In education the ultimate goal is improved student achievement, especially in our nation's cities, where large numbers of students, particularly students of color, are not reaching the levels of achievement they need in order to live successful lives.

There are several implications in play. First, the goal of improved student achievement implies that all children deserve to be successful so improvements need to be made across the entire school system, not just a few schools. Second, it implies responsibility. Measure progress and be accountable. Third, it implies opportunity. A healthy development for our young is the collective responsibility of all civic institutions in a community.

Equity matters. Public education today, sixty some years after *Brown v. Board of Education*, remains highly inequitable. Some children have far more opportunities and resources than others.

Our focus on equity may mean distributing our resources *unequally* because those with the fewest resources often have the greatest need. We need to pay more attention to race, ethnicity, and socioeconomic class as well as individual backgrounds, current patterns of expectation and discrimination. Each affects how children and adults learn and interact with one another.

Communities matter. Because no single institution has a monopoly on expertise and resources, we need the support and resources entire communities can provide. Managing partnerships with parents, taxpayers, municipal officials, youth-serving agencies, philanthropic groups, and local-reform policy makers is hard work. However, making the effort to forge working relationships pays dividends for student achievement.

Learning matters. Education is all about learning. This principle implies that *all* deserve the opportunity to learn what they need to know to be successful. We know the quality of education varies widely from school to school and district to district. We need to design the tools that will enable all schools and districts to create learning communities. Do we need a place where school reformers go to learn? This is food for thought.

The United States has a moral, legal, and civic obligation to deliver high quality education to every child regardless of race, income, or zip code. There are dozens of no-excuses, whatever-it-takes successful schools proving every day that excellence for all is possible.

Many educators today are exploring the notion of "churn," which is rooted in a sense of urgency about needing better schools, rather than an incremental march toward school improvement. Churn involves efforts to transform good schools into great schools. Close the low-performing schools. Open new high-quality schools. Restart "struggling" schools.

Here is the hard part. For "churn" to work, it must include closing persistently low-performing schools that have failed for years to provide high-quality education.

Closing a school, any school, whether district, charter, or private, is difficult. No matter what the challenges, there are often committed teachers, kids who may have been helped, and emotional bonds that have been forged. It is hard for parents to find a new school for their children.

But let's be honest. A school, whether district or charter, with a record of abysmally low proficiency scores and without the value-added evidence of significant growth that indicates students are catching up to grade level, should be closed. We should have the courage to do this because, if we don't, we are dooming its students to failure, not just for school but, potentially for life.

When we look across the country we notice that some urban and rural schools have closed, but it is usually because of organizational restructuring and school consolidation. More needs to be done.

We must encourage charter authorizers as well as district leadership to carefully review their school portfolios, consider the concept of "churn," and see that the difficult decision to close down some of their lowest-performing schools is actually a public service to our children.

The relative decline of American education has long been a national embarrassment as well as a threat to the nation's future. Once upon a time, American students tested better than most students in the world. Now, ranked against European schoolchildren America does about as well as Lithuania, behind at least ten other nations.

For the past fifty years, educators believed that if they could find the right pedagogy, the right instructional method, all would be well. They tried New Math, Whole Language, open classrooms, but nothing gave lasting improvement.

Researchers now say that what matters most is the quality of the teacher. Unfortunately, most teachers today are recruited from the bottom third of college-bound students. At the same time, teacher unions have become more and more powerful. After two or three years teachers are given lifetime tenure. It is virtually impossible to fire them.

Over time many schools, especially in the inner city, succumbed to a defeatist mindset. The problem is not the teacher, it's the parents (or absence thereof), it's society with all its distractions and pathologies, or it's the kids themselves. Not much can be done except to keep the assembly line moving through "social promotion," regardless of academic performance, and hope the students graduate.

By 1990 there was a dramatic achievement gap in the United States, far larger than in other countries, between socioeconomic classes and races. It was a scandal of monumental proportions that there were two distinct school systems in operation, one for middle-class and one for the poor. It will take a quiet revolution to improve American schools.

To the young, schooling seems relentless, but we know it is not. What is relentless is our education, which gives us no rest. That is why poverty is a great educator. Having no boundaries and refusing to be ignored, it mostly teaches helplessness, but not always.

Politics is also a great educator. Mostly it teaches cynicism, but not always. Television is a great educator as well. Mostly it teaches consumerism, but not always. It is the "not always" that keeps the romantic spirit alive in those of us who write about education. We have faith that despite some of the more debilitating teachings of culture itself, something can be done in school that will alter the lenses through which one sees the world.

Education can provide a point of view from which what *is* can be seen clearly, what *was* is a living present, and what *will be* is filled with possibility. Education can be about how to make a life, which is quite different from how to make a living.

When it comes to tracking education, most of the conversation is about means, rarely about ends. Should we privatize our schools? Should we have national standards? How should we use technology? How should we teach reading, math, and on and on?

Some questions spark interest, others do not. It is as if we are a nation of technicians, consumed by our expertise in how something should be done, afraid or incapable of thinking about why. When it comes to learning there is no one who can say that this or that is the best way to know, feel, see, remember, apply, or connect things. Nietzsche's famous aphorism is relevant to all of us: "He who has a *why* to live can bear with almost any *how*."

The idea of public education depends absolutely on the existence of shared narratives and the exclusion of narratives that lead to alienation and divisiveness. There is an old saying among teachers, "All children enter school as question marks and leave as periods." What if we looked at education as an experiment, a perpetual and fascinating question mark?

Let's provide our youth with the knowledge and the will to participate in the great experiment, to teach them how to argue, discover which questions are worth arguing about, and to make sure they know what happens when arguments cease. No one should be excluded from the experiment.

Each of us is thrust into a world that is already in full swing. Our task is to make ourselves into who we want to be while simultaneously fitting ourselves into the world we are constantly constructing. It is not easy being human. In the name of progress we need to blur the distinction between "school life" and "real life," between learning and teaching, and between learning well and living well.

Dwight D. Eisenhower said in 1946, at a commencement address at Gettysburg College, "Fortunately for us and our world, youth is not easily discouraged. . . . The hopes of the world rest on the flexibility, vigor, capacity for new thought, the fresh outlook of the young."

Violence, gangs, racism, drugs, alcohol, sexual promiscuity, and the disintegration of the family are moral issues that cross all racial, cultural, and socioeconomic boundaries. Sooner or later, children everywhere will have to confront these challenges. They can surmount them and go on to lives of purpose with the help of the educational community.

America needs to stop waiting for change to happen and start insisting on it. Then we can transform children's lives and ultimately transform the world.

Equality begins with education.

POINTS TO REMEMBER

- People hold different views on how information is delivered to students.
- Educators need to rethink why we educate.
- Equity, communities, and learning all matter if we want results.
- Consider using the notion of "churn."
- In the name of progress we need to blur the distinction between "school life" and "real life," between learning and teaching, and between learning well and living well.

References

CHAPTER 1

National Geographic. (September 2010). "Poll on Student Geographical Awareness." Washington, DC: National Geographic Society Press.

CHAPTER 2

Coulson, A. (January 2009). "Comparing Public, Private, and Market Schools: The International Evidence." *Journal of School Choice*, pp. 23–29.

CHAPTER 3

Canada, G. (2008). *Whatever It Takes*. New York: Houghton Mifflin.
Gadson, P. (March 2010). "Exposure to A and F." *British Journal of Educational Psychology*, p. 8
Henson, J. (July 27, 2010). "Negative Stereotypes." *Science Daily*, p. 36.
Moen, J. (January 2010). "The Case Against Learning Styles." *Journal of Psychological Science in the Public Interest*, pp. 54–57.

CHAPTER 4

Schott, A. (2010). *Big City Schools Struggle for Survival*. New York: New York Teachers College Press.

120   *References*

CHAPTER 5

Council of Great City Schools. (2010). Report: "A Call for Change." Washington DC: Department of Education Press.

Eric Resources Information Center. (2009). Eric Digest Online.

Schott, A. (2010). *Big City Schools Struggle for Survival.* New York: New York Teachers College Press.

CHAPTER 6

Justice Policy Institute. (2011). *Cell Blocks or Classrooms? The Funding of Education and Corrections and Its Impact.* Washington DC: Justice Policy Institute Publishing.

National Clearinghouse for English Language Acquisition. (2010). "Immigration Counts." Washington DC: U.S. Department of Education.

United States Census Bureau. (1995). Yearly Report on ELLs. Washington DC: Bureau Press.

CHAPTER 7

Merrow, J. (July 6, 2011). "Who influences American education today?" Blog atwww.huggingtonpost.com/johnmerrow.

Murray, C. (October 25, 2010). "Class and Culture, Murray's New Elitism." *Washington Post.*

CHAPTER 9

Murray, L. (March 17, 2011). "Educating Poor Minority Children." *New Republic* 242 (14), pp. 41–43.

CHAPTER 10

Seidel, S. (July 22, 2010). Interview.